W9-BXX-804

GARDENS

edited and with an introduction by
MERILYN SIMONDS

GARDENS

A LITERARY COMPANION

 David Suzuki Foundation

GREYSTONE BOOKS
DOUGLAS & MCINTYRE PUBLISHING GROUP
VANCOUVER/TORONTO/BERKELEY

For Ida Feher

Greystone Books
A division of Douglas & McIntyre Ltd.
2323 Quebec Street, Suite 201
Vancouver BC Canada V5T 4S7
www.greystonebooks.com

David Suzuki Foundation
219–2211 West 4th Avenue
Vancouver BC Canada V6K 4S2

Library and Archives Canada Cataloguing in Publication
Gardens : a literary companion / edited and with an introduction
by Merilyn Simonds ; series editor Wayne Grady.
(Greystone natural wonders series)
Co-published by the David Suzuki Foundation.

ISBN 978-1-55365-327-1

1. Gardens—Literary collections. 2. Gardening—
Literary collections. I. Simonds, Merilyn, 1949– II. Grady, Wayne
III. David Suzuki Foundation. IV. Series.
PN6071.G27G375 2008   808.84'9364   C2007-905324-6

Jacket and text design by Peter Cocking
Jacket images © Veer Incorporated
Printed and bound in Canada by Friesens
Printed on acid-free paper that is forest friendly (100% post-consumer
recycled paper) and has been processed chlorine free.
Distributed in the U.S. by Publishers Group West

We gratefully acknowledge the financial support of the Canada Council for the Arts,
the British Columbia Arts Council, the Province of British Columbia through the
Book Publishing Tax Credit, and the Government of Canada through the Book Publishing
Industry Development Program (BPIDP) for our publishing activities.

CONTENTS

INTRODUCTION

GARDENS STRADDLE THE DIVIDE between Nature and human nature. This is literally so: the word "garden" comes from the Old English *geard* (as in "yard"), which means enclosure, a space that is bounded, set apart, usually to one side of a house. The garden is at once attached to domesticity and, at the same time, part of the natural world, one that must be walled lest it vanish into wilderness.

The garden, in fact, marks a vital turning point in our species' history. We began as mammals on the move, hunters and gatherers of food. The moment we poked seeds into the ground to make a stalk of grain or a melon grow where we wanted it to, instead of where it sprouted of its own accord, we set ourselves on the civilizing path. Because of that first garden, we could put down roots, build a house, raise a family, gather other families around, so that those of us good at growing corn and fruit could trade our harvest with those who could whip a bearskin into a coat. Without the garden, we'd still be wandering the wilds in search of nuts and berries, instead of making the nuts and berries come to us.

Because it was the first thing we enclosed and made our own, the garden has become a symbol of the human penchant for control. At the same time, it is a living lesson in the futility of such an aspiration, as I learned in my years of gardening on the northern edge of Ontario's Algonquin Park. A plot of land left unattended for a season would soon sprout alder and black willow, sumac, then birch, the evergreens would spring up, and within a decade, only a staunch lilac or a twist of *Rosa rugosa* remained to give evidence that a garden once flourished there.

Indeed, the wall that defines a garden is mostly etymological. In real life, a garden remains wedded to the natural world. "A true garden," writes Douglas Chambers in his horticultural memoir, *Stonyground*, "is never apart from its landscape. It arises from it like Eve from Adam's rib; it makes love to the fields in the language of botany." This is true even for the high-walled gardens of rural Italy and France. A plant may stay put, but it flings its fragrance and seeds into the street. Pollen hitches a ride on the hairy ankles of bees. Lilies of the valley send their shoots scouting under fences; vines scale the heights and tumble over walls. "Our gardens," observed Colette, "told each other everything."

It is that enduring connection with Nature that draws us into the garden, whether the plants are nurtured on a high-rise balcony or on the thirty acres that Francis Bacon, in his essay excerpted here, deems the proper size for what he calls "the purest of human pleasures." My earliest photographic portrait dates from when I was three, hoisting a tin watering can over my grandmother's vegetables. From the childish joy of witnessing the miraculous metamorphosis of a tiny beadlike seed into a round, fat cabbage grew the adult desire to know each plant, its habits, its preferences, its various names and aliases, its uses in the natural world and in our own. With an understanding of the complexities of Nature inevitably comes an appreciation of its ruthless whimsy. Try as I might to control the soil, the moisture, the microclimate of my own bits of enclosed earth, still drought shrivels the peas, hail beats down the Shirley poppies, and rain washes the lettuce seed into the gutters where it sprouts into thick green mats. As the great American garden writer Allen Lacy concludes in "Invasion of the Sumac," gardens keep us humble.

Writers have been harvesting the garden for metaphors of the human condition since the first stylus scratched papyrus. In the Old Testament of the Christian Bible, among the most ancient of religious books, God is characterized as the first gardener and Eden the first garden, one we were banished from for breaking the rules. In Greek mythology, the garden of the Hesperides grew golden apples that offered immortality; by awarding one to Aphrodite, Paris precipitated the fall of Troy. When Cadmus sowed a row of dragon's teeth, warriors sprang out of the earth to kill him. It was in the garden of Gethsemane that Jesus was betrayed.

Gardens are not always such dangerous places, but neither are they the carnivals portrayed in Bosch's *Garden of Earthly Delights*. More often, gardens are lovely places, like the tranquil garden where Dushyanta, the handsome king of Indian myth, first saw the beautiful, wise Shakuntala. In Shakespearean comedies, gardens are sites of magical transformation. In Japan, the garden is a symbol of peace, particularly so, the tea gardens that house the intricate ceremonies of the tea masters, developed in the sixteenth century. Indeed, poets through the ages have extolled the garden as the epitome of beauty, of enduring love, of indefatigable, ever-renewing passion. As Thomas Moore put it, "The soul cannot thrive in the absence of a garden."

Perhaps gardens are a lodestone for writers because, like writing, a garden is essentially an act of the imagination. It lives in its most perfect form in the mind and heart, not only of the person who makes it, but of those who stroll through it, and those who carry it away in their thoughts and memories. That is the allure, no doubt, of Nebuchadnezzar's long-vanished Hanging Gardens of Babylon, one of the seven wonders of the ancient world, which live on in the imagination twenty-five hundred years after they were built, though no detailed description exists.

"The garden is a ground plot for the mind," wrote Thomas Hill five hundred years ago in *The Gardener's Labyrinth*, England's first gardening book, a dictum that was taken to heart by Napoleon's wife, Josephine. Uprooted from her tropical paradise of Martinique, she became an obsessive gardener, amassing the largest collection of roses eighteenth-century Europe had ever seen and introducing to her adopted home the eucalyptus, hibiscus, dahlias, and jasmine to remind her of the place she'd come from. Two hundred years later, Jamaica Kincaid, another Caribbean transplant, this time to the United States, makes the same point: "My garden is for me an exercise in memory," she notes in the introduction to *My Garden (Book):*, "a way of remembering my own immediate past, a way of getting to a past that is my own (the Caribbean Sea) and the past as it is indirectly related to me."

Writers and gardens are so intertwined that a collection of poems, prayers, and other literary works was once known by the Latin word for garden, *hortus:* the commonplace book compiled by the abbess Herrad in the twelfth century, for example, was called the *Hortus deliciarum,* or *Garden of Delights.* Robert Louis Stevenson continued the tradition with *A Child's Garden of Verses.* A collection of writing today is still called an anthology, which derives from two Greek words: *anthos* (flowers) and *logy* (to speak of). When "anthology" was first used in English, during the time of Francis Bacon and John Gerard, it applied specifically to a gathering of small choice poems; eventually, it came to mean to any thoughtful harvest of literary writing.

Gardens: A Literary Companion is a garden of gardens, then, a gleaning of some of the finest writing about the cultivated natural world. These twenty-eight essays start in the garden and meander across time and space and along the endless paths of human curiosity and inspiration. Here is Tim Smit stumbling upon the remains of Heligan, a four-hundred-year-old garden lost amid the brambles of Cornwall; Midge Ellis Keeble digging into her suburban yard and finding Eden; the nineteenth-century Irish novelist Emily Lawless contemplating the necessity of weeds; lyrical poet Elizabeth Smart attempting to supplant rampant nettledom with a Wondrous Watery Realm. French artist Henri Cueco debates beauty with his gardener, while

Thomas Hardy's gardener gives us a unique view of the man known as the last great Victorian writer. Ernest Wilson travels to the China-Tibet border to find the regal lily, Jamaica Kincaid strolls through Monet's garden, Colette decries the *jardins prisonniers* of Paris, Lewis Gannett visits the accidental gardens of bombed-out London, Vita Sackville-West ponders the Transvaal daisy, and John Gerard enthuses over the potato. For Karel Capek, Des Kennedy, and Germaine Greer (writing as Rose Blight), gardens are fertile ground for poking fun. For Eleanor Perenyi, a shrub of blowsy peonies becomes the provocateur that sends her to the bookshelf wondering, where did it come from? Why is one single, another double? Why do none of them smell, as Colette said they did, of cockchafers? For Patrick Lane, the questions are more philosophical. Observing a squirrel attacking his bird feeder, he admits, "I have given up driving her away and now accept she has her own needs. What am I trying to save, a handful a day of sunflower seeds? I let her have her due."

The pieces in this literary companion to the garden were selected and organized according to the same principles that pertain in my own garden: each delights on its own merits, and when enjoyed with those in close proximity, gives fuller satisfaction, while the deepest pleasure comes from sitting back and contemplating the subtle interplay of these cultivated reflections of the natural world.

MERILYN SIMONDS

BRINGING HOME
THE REGAL LILY

ERNEST H. WILSON

Ernest H. Wilson (1876–1930) began work as a gardener at age sixteen. Later employed at Kew Gardens, London, he was sent on his first plant-hunting trip to China in 1899, returning again in 1903. From these two trips, he brought back specimens and seed from two thousand different plants. After moving to Boston to become Keeper at the Arnold Arboretum, he made further expeditions to Japan, Formosa, New Zealand, and Africa. Credited with introducing more than a thousand species into cultivation, Wilson called China the "mother of gardens." Never glaciated, it harbors the richest accumulation of temperate flora in the world, nourishing nearly an eighth of the world's plant species and contributing more than half of the ornamental plants in our gardens, including this unmistakably regal lily.

. . .

JOURNEY IN THOUGHT with me for a moment or two, westward, until "west" becomes "east," although we still chase the setting sun. Across the broad American continent, across that wide ocean misnamed "Pacific," to Shanghai, gate of Far

Cathay; onward and westward up the mighty Yangtsze River for 1800 miles, then northward up its tributary the Min, some 250 miles to the confines of mysterious Thibet; to that little-known hinterland which separates China proper from the hierarchy of Lhassa; to a wild and mountainous country peopled mainly by strange tribesfolks of unknown origin; to a land where Lamaism, Buddhism and Phallism strive for mastery of men's souls; to a region where mighty empires meet. There in narrow, semiarid valleys, down which torrents thunder, and encompassed by mountains composed of mud-shales and granites whose peaks are clothed with snow eternal, the Regal Lily has her home. In summer the heat is terrific, in winter the cold is intense, and at all seasons these valleys are subject to sudden and violent windstorms against which neither man nor beast can make headway. There in June, by the way side, in rock-crevice by the torrent's edge and high up on the mountainside and precipice, this Lily in full bloom greets the weary wayfarer. Not in twos and threes but in hundreds, in thousands, aye, in tens of thousands. Its slender stems, each from 2 to 4 feet tall, flexible and tense as steel, overtop the coarse grasses and scrub and are crowned with one to several large funnel-shaped flowers, each more or less wine-colored without, pure white and lustrous on the face, clear canary-yellow within the tube and each stamen filament tipped with a golden anther. The air in the cool of the morning and in the evening is laden with delicious perfume exhaled from every blossom. For a brief season this Lily transforms a lonely, semi-desert region into a veritable fairyland.

Sungpang Ting is a military town situated on the head-waters of the Min River on the very edge of the grasslands of northeastern Thibet. It is a very important outpost of Chinese civilization and a trade entreport of considerable magnitude. Medicines in great variety, including the famous Rhubarb and Musk, are brought in by tribesfolk from the neighboring mountains and bartered to Chinese merchants. I knew the town well and on former occasions had rested within its walls and beneath the clear blue skies it enjoys had recuperated after arduous journeys. So, too, on this occasion. Rested and re-provisioned I and my followers sallied forth and for seven consecutive days plunged down the seemingly interminable gorge of the Min River. The mountains on either side are so high that the summits were usually hidden from view. Here and there where some tributary stream flows in, a glimpse of snow eternal met our gaze. Habitations are few and far between but wherever possible patches of the mountainside are under agriculture. It was frightfully hot and travelling was most fatiguing. In many places the narrow track is hewn and blasted from the solid rock and here and there tunnelling has been necessary. In several places Chinese characters of huge size carved in the rocks warn those who can interpret them of the dangers of the road and urge all not to tarry in particular places. This road, difficult and narrow as it is, is the artery of ingress and egress to Sungpang Ting from and to the cities of wealthy Szechuan. There was in consequence much traffic, largely coolies, but several mule-trains taking up brick-tea and cotton cloth in particular, and various merchandise in general and bringing down medicines, hides and deer horns. The road is narrow, sometimes it skirts the edge of the river's turbulent waters but more usually ribbon-like it winds along from fifty to 300 feet above. The passing of mule-trains is a difficult business, often possible only at particular places when one caravan comes to a standstill and allows the other to pass.

I travelled mostly on foot but had with me a light sedan chair made of rattan and my Boy or principal servant was similarly favored. A sedan chair is an outward and visible sign of respectability without which no traveller is properly equipped. In those days it was of far more importance than a passport, for it inspired confidence and insured the respect of the people. Whether one rode in it or walked was immaterial; the important thing was its presence.

On the seventh day we were down to 5500 feet altitude and the following extract from my diary seems worth recording: "A bad road through barren, desolate country and abnormally long miles sums up the day's journey. Barring absolute desert no more barren and repelling country could be imagined than that traversed today. But it is really only the narrow valley and precipitous mountainsides that are so desertlike. On the upper slopes trees and cultivation occur and small villages and farm-houses are frequent. In the valley houses are far between and what few there are are in ruinous condition. A fierce up-river wind blows regularly from about eleven o'clock in the morning and it is difficult to make headway against it. The leaves on the Maize plants are torn to shreds by the wind's violence. The

Regal Lily occurs here and there in abundance on the well-nigh stark slate and mudstone cliffs."

The eighth day I camped and for several days was busy arranging to secure in October, the proper season of the year, some six or seven thousand bulbs of the Regal Lily. Plans completed we set out for Chengtu Fu, the capital city of Szechuan. The hardship of a four months' journey were beginning to tell on me and dysentery in a mild form had troubled me for days. Yet it was with a light heart and a satisfied mind that I rode in my chair. Soon after starting we passed a mule-train breaking camp and bound our way. With the thoughts of the flesh pots of Chengtu Fu only four days' distance, all were in a cheerful mood. We were making good progress, my chair leading, with personal attendants and man carrying my large camera immediately behind; my black spaniel dog wagging his tail ahead of us all. The Chinese characters of warning carved in the rocks did not afright us, we had seen so many and passed all well. Song was in our hearts, when I noticed my dog suddenly cease wagging his tail, cringe and rush forward and a small piece of rock hit the path and rebounded into the river some 300 feet below us. I shouted an order and the bearers put down the chair. The two front bearers ran forward and I essayed to follow suit. Just as I cleared the chair-handles a large boulder crashed into the body of the chair and down to the river it was hurled. I ran, instinctively ducked as something whisked over my head and my sun hat blew off. Again I ran, a few yards more and I would be under the lea of some hard rocks. Then feeling as if a hot wire passed through my leg, I was bowled over, tried to jump up, found my right leg was useless, so crawled forward to the shelter of the cliff, where the two scared chair-bearers were huddled.

It was only a small slide and our lives had had a providential escape. The man carrying my camera could not run back so fast as others and suffered a bad scalp wound. I was the biggest sufferer but, fortunately, was not knocked unconscious. If I had been the men would probably have deserted from fright, as it was they behaved well. The pigskin puttee on my right leg was cut slantingly as with a knife and forced round my leg, the toe cap of my boot was torn off and with it the nail of my big toe; the right leg was broken in two places below the knee and the side of my calf was badly lacerated. Not a pleasant situation to find oneself in alone with Chinese and four days from the nearest medical assistance!

As soon as it was safe to do so the men came along, terrified and solicitous. My Boy with his chair also came soon afterward but was quite ignorant of the whole affair. With the legs of my camera tripod I improvised splints and while these were being bandaged to my leg the mule-caravan passed in the morning loomed into view. The road was too narrow for them to turn back and they dare not stand still until I could be moved forward, since we knew not when the rock slide would re-commence. There was only one thing to do. I lay across the road and the mules stepped over my body. Then it was that I realized the size of the mule's hoof. There were nearer fifty than forty of them and each stepped clearly over me as if accustomed to such obstacles. Nevertheless, I breathed freely when the last was over!

My own chair being smashed I requisitioned the Boy's, had a piece of wood laid cross-wise and lashed the leg in splints to the right pole. At considerable risk to themselves the men salvaged my wrecked chair and we started on our journey to Chengtu Fu. We made it in three days, marching early and late, and three agonizing days they were for me. At Chengtu Fu I was carried to the house of Mr. Davidson of the Friends' Presbyterian Mission and all that could be done was done. The leg had become infected. In spite of every care, at the end of six weeks there was no signs of the bones uniting. The question of amputation was pressed but somehow I never felt this would be necessary. Other doctors were called in, including a French army surgeon named Dr. Mouillac. Some cutting and slitting was done and the infection stayed. At the end of three months I was out on crutches. Soon afterward I hired a boat and started down the river toward Ichang, where steamers were available for Shanghai and thence for America. At every place on the river where there were medical missionaries I received attention. On crutches I crossed the Pacific Ocean and the American continent to spend a couple of weeks in a hospital in Boston, Massachusetts. Afterward, fitted with a special boot I was able to limp about with a cane and in just a year from the date of the accident walked freely once again. Owing to the infection it was impossible to fit the leg in a cast and so the bones just grew together. The leg is crooked, fifteen-sixteenths of an inch short but is strong and sound and has since carried me many, many thousands of miles.

The accident notwithstanding, I got my Regal Lily and brought the bulbs safely to Boston. The arrangements I had made with the local peasantry to dig the bulbs were carried out under the supervision of my trained collectors. The bulbs were encased in clay, packed in charcoal, shipped at silk rates, and reached Boston a few days after myself. Planted in a garden in Roslindale, Massacheusetts, they flowered freely in the June following and some even ripened seeds. From this stock has sprung the millions now happily acclimated in American gardens and other gardens across the seas. Its beauty captured all hearts at sight. Its merits have been lauded far and wide by many scribes. It loves this country and the climate and from the Atlantic to the Pacific is grown wherever gardens are loved. Each year it adds to the pleasure of millions of folk. The price I paid has been stated. The Regal Lily was worth it and more.

THE TRANSVAAL DAISY

VITA SACKVILLE-WEST

Vita Sackville-West (1892–1962) was a prolific English poet, dramatist, and essayist throughout her life. In 1913, she married diplomat and critic Harold Nicolson, with whom she lived first in Persia, then at Sissinghurst, a derelict Kentish castle they restored and beautified with gardens that have become a destination for gardeners worldwide. Her love affairs, principally with Virginia Woolf, often overshadow her twin abiding passions of literature and horticulture. For fourteen years, she wrote a weekly garden column for *The Observer,* where she promulgated her three principles of ruthlessness, untidiness (let self-seeded plants grow where they will), and vision (have an architectural plan, a color plan, and a seasonal plan). *Some Flowers* (1937), the first of her nine gardening books, is a charming collection of imaginative essays about her favorite plants.

. . .

THERE ARE SOME flowers about which there is nothing interesting to say, except that they happen to have caught one's fancy. Such a flower, so far as I am concerned, is *Gerbera jamesonii*. It has no historical interest that I know of; no long record of danger and difficulty attending its discovery, no background of savage mountains and Asiatic climates. It carries, in fact, no romantic appeal at all. It has taken no man's life. It has to stand or fall on its own merits.

I first observed it in the window of a florist's shop, neatly rising out of a gilt basket tied with pink ribbons. No more repellant presentation could be imagined, or anything more likely to put one against the flower for ever, yet somehow this poor ill-treated flower struck me instantly as a lovely thing, so lovely that I suffered on its behalf to see it so misunderstood. I went in to enquire its name, but the young lady assistant merely gaped at me, as they nearly always do if one makes any enquiry about their wares unconnected with their price. It was only later, at a flower-show, that I discovered it to be *Gerbera jamesonii*, also called the Transvaal daisy. Neither name pleased me very much, but the flower itself pleased me very much indeed. It seemed to include every colour one could most desire, especially a coral pink and a rich yellow, and every petal as shiny and polished as a buttercup. Long, slender stalks and a clean erect habit. It was altogether a very clean looking flower; in fact it might have been freshly varnished.

The exhibitor was better informed than the florist's young lady. It was only hardy in this country, he said, if it could be grown in very dry conditions at the foot of a warm wall, in which case it might be regarded as a reasonably hardy perennial.

I know however that nurserymen are frequently more optimistic in their recommendations than they should be, so privately resolved to grow it in an unheated greenhouse. This house is really a long lean-to, sloped against the brick wall of an old stable, and all along the foot of the wall runs a bed about six feet wide, which is an ideal place for growing things such as the Gerbera which cannot without a certain anxiety be left out-of-doors. I wonder indeed why those who were fortunate enough to possess such a lean-to, do not more frequently put it to this use. It is true that it entails sacrificing all the staging down one side of the house, but the gain is great. Staging means pots, and pots mean watering, and "potting on" if you are to avoid root-starvation, whereas plants set straight into the ground can root down to Australia if they like. You can moreover make up the soil to suit every separate kind; you can work under cover in bad weather; you can snap your fingers at hailstorms, late frosts, young rabbits, and even, to a certain extent, slugs. There is certainly a great deal to be said for this method of gardening.

I once saw a lean-to house which had been adapted in this way, with a special view to growing lilies. The wall had been distempered in a light blue, of that peculiar shade produced by spraying vines with copper sulphate against the walls of farmhouses in Italy: in the centre was a sunk rectangular pool, with blue nympheae growing in it and clumps of agapanthus at each of the four corners. The tall lilies rose straight and pure and pale against the curious blue of the wall. I liked best going into this house after dark, when the single electric reflector in the roof cast down a flood-lighting effect more unreal and unearthly than anything I had ever seen.

At least, let me be strictly truthful. I never really saw this lean-to house at all. I only heard it discussed, before it had materialised. And then it grew in my mind, turning into the thing I wanted it to be. In my mind, I added the pool, and the spraying with copper sulphate, and the flood-lighting, and the pale lilies. It was ideally lovely, as I imagined it. Perhaps it has materialised since then, perhaps it has not. I almost hope it has not.

MONET'S GARDEN

JAMAICA KINCAID

Jamaica Kincaid (1949–) was born in Antigua as Elaine Potter Richard-
son, a name she changed when, after moving to New York to work as
an *au pair*, she became a published author. A staff writer for the *New Yorker*
from 1976 to 1995, Kincaid is also a noted novelist, essayist, and mem-
oirist. A recent book, *Among Flowers: A Walk in the Himalaya* (2005), is
her account of a plant-hunting trip to Nepal. This selection comes from
My Garden (Book):, a collection of essays spun from her Vermont garden.
Obsessed in her fiction with the destruction of paradise, Kincaid's relationship to her garden is complex and fraught, restless, fervent, and intensely
playful. "How agitated I am when I am in the garden," she writes, "and
how happy I am to be so agitated."

.   .   .

WHAT WOULD THE GARDEN be without the paintings?
Would I be standing in it (the garden, Claude Monet's garden),
looking at the leaf-green arches on which were trained roses

("American Pillar," "Dainty Bess," "Paul's Scarlet Rambler")
and clematis ("Montana Rubens"), looking at the beds of opium
poppies, Oriental poppies, looking at the sweep of bearded iris
(they had just passed bloom), looking at dottings of fat peonies
(plants only, they had just passed bloom), and looking at roses
again, this time standardized, in bloom in that way of the paintings (the real made to shimmer as if it will vanish from itself, the
real made to seem so nearby and at the same time so far away)?

It was June. I was standing looking at the *Solanum* "Optical Illusion" (Monet himself grew the species *Solanum retonii*
but *Solanum* "Optical Illusion" is what I saw on a label placed
next to this plant) and the hollyhock "Zebrina" (they were in
bloom in all their simple straightforwardness, their uncompli-
cated mauve-colored petals streaked with lines of purple, and
this color purple seemed innocent of doubt); looking at the
other kind of hollyhock, *Alcea rosea,* which was only in bud,
so I could not surreptitiously filch the seedpods; looking at the
yellow-flowering thalictrum, the poppies again (only this time
they were field poppies, *Papaver rhoeas,* and they were in a
small area to the side of the arches of roses, but you can't count
on them being there from year to year, for all the poppies sow
themselves wherever they want); looking at an area of lawn set
off by apple trees trained severely along a fence made of wire
painted green and beech posts.

I was looking at all these things, but I had their counterparts
in Monet's paintings in my mind. It was June, so I had missed
the lawn full of blooming daffodils and fritillarias, they came

in the spring. And all this was only the main part of the garden, separate from the water garden, famous for the water lilies, the wisteria growing over the Japanese bridge, the Hoschedé girls in a boat.

And would the water garden be the same without the paintings? On the day (days) I saw it, the water garden—that is, the pond with lilies growing in it—the Hoschedé girls were not standing in a boat on the pond, for they have been dead for a very long time now, and if I expected them to appear standing in the boat, it is only because the pond itself looked so familiar, like the paintings, shimmering (that is sight), enigmatic (that is feeling, or what you say about feeling when you mean many things), and new (which is what you say about something you have no words for yet, good or bad, accept or reject: "It's new!")—yes, yes, so familiar from the paintings.

But when I saw the water garden itself (the real thing, the thing that Monet himself had first made and the thing that has become only a memory of what he had made after he was no longer there to care about it, he had been dead a long time by then), it had been restored and looked without doubt like the thing Monet had made, a small body of water manipulated by him, its direction coming from a natural source, a nearby stream. On the day I saw it, the pond, the Hoschedé girls (all three of them) were not in a boat looking so real that when they were seen in that particular painting (*The Boat at Giverny*) they would then define reality. The Hoschedé girls were not there, for they had long been dead also, and in fact, there were no girls in a boat

on the pond, only a woman, and she was in a boat and holding
a long-handled sieve, skimming debris from the surface of the
pond. The pond itself (and this still is on the day that I saw it)
was in some flux, water was coming in or water was going out,
I could not really tell (and I did not really want to know). The
water lilies were lying on their sides, their roots exposed to clear
air, but on seeing them that way I immediately put them back
in the arrangement I am most familiar with them in the paintings, sitting in the water that is the canvas with all their begin-
nings and all their ends hidden from me. The wisteria growing
over the Japanese bridge was so familiar to me (again), and how
very unprepared I was to see that its trunk had rotted out and
was hollow and looked ravaged, and ravaged is not what Monet
evokes in anyone looking at anything associated with him (even
in the painting he made of Camille, his wife before Alice, dead,
she does not look ravaged, only dead, as if to be dead is only
another way to exist). But to see these things—the wisteria, the
Japanese bridge, the water lilies, the pond itself (especially the
pond, for here the pond looks like a canvas)—is to be suddenly
in a whirl of feelings. For here is the real thing, the real material
thing: wisteria, water lily, pond, Japanese bridge—in its proper
setting, a made-up landscape in Giverny, made up by the gardener Claude Monet. And yet I see these scenes now because I
had seen them the day before in a museum (the Musée d'Orsay)
and the day before that in another museum (the Musée Marmot-
tan) and many days and many nights (while lying in bed) before
that, in books, and it is the impression of them (wisteria, water

lily, pond, Japanese bridge) that I had seen in these other ways before (the paintings in the museums, the reproductions in the books) that gave them a life, a meaning outside the ordinary.

A garden will die with its owner, a garden will die with the death of the person who made it. I had this realization one day while walking around in the great (and even worthwhile) effort that is Sissinghurst, the garden made by Vita Sackville-West and her husband, Harold Nicolson. Sissinghurst is extraordinary: it has all the impersonal beauty of a park (small), yet each part of it has the intimacy of a garden—a garden you could imagine creating yourself if only you were so capable. And then again to see how a garden will die with the gardener, you have only to look at Monet's friend and patron Gustave Caillebotte; the garden he made at Petit Gennevilliers no longer exists; the garden in Yerres, where he grew up, the one depicted in some of his paintings, is mostly in disarray. When I saw the potagerie, the scene that is the painting, *Yerres, in the Kitchen Garden: Gardeners Watering the Plants* was now a dilapidated forest of weeds: a cat who looked as if it belonged to no one stared crossly at me; a large tin drum stood just where you might expect to see a gardener, barefoot and carrying two watering cans. The Yerres River itself no longer seemed wide and deep and mysteriously shimmering (as in *Boater Pulling In his Périssoire, Banks of the Yerres* or *Bathers, Banks of the Yerres*), it was now only ordinarily meandering, dirty, like any old memory.

And so, would the garden, in Giverny, in which I was standing one day in early June, mean so much to me and all the other people traipsing around without the paintings? The painting *The Artist's Garden at Giverny* is in a museum in Connecticut, the painting *The Flowering Arches* is in a museum in Arizona, the painting *The Japanese Footbridge* is in a museum in Houston. *Water Lilies* are everywhere. On seeing them, these paintings, either in the setting of a museum or reproduced in a book, this gardener can't help but long to see the place they came from, the place that held the roses growing up the arches, the pond in which the lilies grew, the great big path (called the Grand Allée) that led from the front door of the house and divided the garden in two, the weeping willow, the Japanese bridge, the gladiolas (they were not yet in bloom when I was there), the peonies (they were past bloom when I was there), the dahlias (they were not yet in bloom when I was there).

That very same garden that he (Monet) made does not exist; that garden died, too, the way gardens do when their creators and sustainers disappear. And yet the garden at Giverny that he (Monet) made is alive in the paintings, and the person seeing the paintings (and that would be anyone, really) can't help but wonder where they came from, what the things in the painting were really like in their vegetable and animal (physical) form. In the narrative that we are in (the Western one), the word comes before the picture; the word makes us long for a picture, the word is never enough for the thing just seen—the picture!

The garden that Monet made has been restored to itself, has been restored so that when we look at it, there is no discrepancy, it is just the way we remember it (but this must be the paintings), it is just the way it should be. As I was standing there in June (nearby were tray upon tray of Ageratum seedlings about to be planted out in a bedding), a man holding a camera (and he was the very definition of confidence) said to me, "Monet knew exactly what he was doing." I did not say to him that people who know exactly what they are doing always end up with exactly what they are doing.

The house at Giverny in which he (Monet) lived has also been restored. It can be seen, a tour of the house and garden is available. As I was going through the rooms of the house—the yellow dining room, the blue kitchen, the bedrooms with the beds all properly made up, the drawing room with prints of scenes and people from Japan—I hurried, I rushed through. I felt as if at any moment now, the occupant, the owner (Monet, whoever it might be) would return and I would be caught looking into someone's private life. I would be caught in a place I was not really meant to be.

THE GREEN SHROUD

TIM SMIT

Tim Smit (1954–) worked as an archaeologist before becoming a song-writer and millionaire music producer. In 1987, he retired to Cornwall where, under the bramble bushes next door, he discovered the remains of sumptuous gardens dating back to the twelfth century. *The Lost Gardens of Heligan* tells the restoration tale of what has now become a top British tour-ist attraction. Awarded the Companion of the British Empire in 2002, Smit has gone on to create the Eden Project, a "living theatre" of plants housed under huge transparent biomes constructed in an old Cornish china-clay quarry. A self-professed maverick, Smit's mission, he says, is to change the world into one where "plants provide a canvas on which we can paint an optimistic future."

. . .

IT WAS THE SILENCE, the unearthly silence that struck you first. Some silences have a stillness to them, a calm that suggests a moment of life at rest, but this was a silence that vested every-thing with a deep, brooding melancholy. Gradually, it dawned on you: you could hear no birdsong, no rustlings, nor even the far-off murmur of life elsewhere. Even the wind seemed to hold its breath, the only sound a faint and distant creaking, like the settling timbers of a ship at anchor.

This dank, dark place had its own strange beauty. We had cut our way through what we later discovered had once been a formal laurel hedge, grown to shield the pleasure grounds from those who had used the main drive to the big house. The hedge had grown massive and now stretched at least thirty yards in width. Here, in this underworld, the laurel trunks arched and writhed, contorted into a Medusa's fringe of unimaginable shapes. I had never seen such boughs before. It wasn't just their size, though that was impressive enough, some of the main stems being thicker than a man's thigh. It was also the velvety feel of them, like a new stag's horn. Starved of sun for so long, they played host to legions of algae in a startling palette of colours, from lime green through orange to blue-black.

Having crawled on hands and knees, climbed, cut, pulled and pushed our way through to the far side of the hedge, we had to let our eyes adjust to the daylight and reflect on the sight that greeted us. There were brambles snaking everywhere. Thickly matted to chest height, they ensnared all the trees and shrubs, at times seeming to defy gravity as they arched across open space like angel hair on a Christmas tree. Poking through this sea of thorns were some amazing plants; huge rhododendrons, what appeared to be palm trees, indeterminate evergreens, all framed by massive, still living trees keeled over like drunks.

I had never given much thought to brambles before, except when blackberry picking. You could not help but admire the pioneering spirit of the plant, its shading so successful that none but the hardiest of competitors could thrive in what little light it left behind. Underneath its blanket was the stench of decay, the only survivors shade-loving ferns and those plants that were tall enough to escape its hungry embrace and reach for the sun. In most cases even they were disfigured, looking like tall tribesmen with rickety legs and big hair.

We exercised the greatest caution as we cut our way through the unending bramble patch, punctuated by what appeared to be an avenue of palm trees with a line of tall evergreens as a backcloth. The oldest brambles were woody and as thick as your thumb, and quite capable of inflicting serious injury on the unwary. A too-casual sweep of the machete could lead to it bouncing off, or the bramble snapping with a sound like a whiplash and flashing past your face, leaving you to reflect humbly on the importance of your eyesight.

Our plan was to cut from one side to the other so as to give ourselves a sense of scale for what we were looking at. In due course we found ourselves at the foot of an enormous oak tree, where at last the brambles began to relent. In the bole of the tree we heard a low humming, which was unusual in itself. We peered up, to be transfixed by the sight of the most enormous wasps I have ever had the misfortune to come across. To my phobic imagination they were at least two inches long and looked like evil incarnate.

We found good reason to hurry away from this place, and plunged through some straggly laurels to find ourselves on what might have been a path; by looking up at the sky, we could make out an avenue of palms and rhododendrons through which our route meandered. We cut our way through with renewed vigour, only to find our path blocked by a massive tree, its trunk at least six feet across. It was still alive, its branches apparently impenetrable. As we inched along it we could just make out exotic fern-like plants and a tantalizing, brilliant flash of colour from an early-flowering rhododendron. But we couldn't get through.

I had only just met John Willis, but this moment created the bond. In desperation we retraced our steps with the idea of finding a new route round the tree. As we hurried John remarked that there appeared to be a stone edging underfoot. All of a sudden we could see what looked like a rockery, its rough-hewn stones crowned with enormous rhododendrons and the exotic fern-like plants we'd seen in the glade beyond the fallen tree. We were drawn down the path and found ourselves back in deep shade, descending what must once have been steps, although they were buried well beneath the debris. We kept our balance by holding on to the rockery stones which led, to our amazement, to the mouth of a cave. Its beautifully corbelled entrance arch was veiled by drooping laurel branches growing out of the roof. Inside it was wet and cold, the walls and ceiling covered in mould. A curved stone bench seat lined the wall, most of it buried under a thick cushion of loam. This was obviously a trysting spot of old . . . or were we being hopelssly romantic?

Beyond the cave the narrow path meandered through a range of moss-covered rockeries until we came upon a well, set into the face of one of them. It was flooded, and what appeared to be an ornate Gothic capstone lay face down in the water in front of it. The whole structure was simply built and covered in moss, giving it the appearance of great age.

We walked on from the well, ducked under some fallen trees and found ourselves looking, bizarrely, at a modern hardcore road, driven through with no concern for the plants. Piles of earth, splintered trees and shrubs, a mountain of debris; who-ever had done this had no idea that there was a garden here at all. We traced the entire route and found that it cut from the main drive through to parkland. It was nothing more than a farm track.

The spell was broken, and we were all set to retrace our steps back to the real world. But something else caught our attention. From the track we could make out, through mountainous rho-dodendrons, the outline of a structure. On drawing closer we could see a large brick wall with what must once have been working buildings set against it. They were almost gutted, their timbers rotten, yet these ruins had a resonance, an all-pervading sense of sadness, that captivated the imagination. Gingerly, not wanting to bring the walls down, we crept into one of them, and found, behind some fallen roof slates, an old stokehole, with a boiler set at the bottom of a flight of steps. A doorway led into a tiny room with a broken window and a fireplace, inside which we could still make out the kettle-hooks. Poking out from under the debris was the old kettle, rusted and knobbly with the accretions of years spent waiting for its next call to service.

Back outside, our spirits much lifted, we faced the ruins of a glasshouse of unlikely proportions, so small one couldn't imagine being able to grow anything in it whatsoever. Next to it was a large wooden door that led, we supposed, to the other side of the great wall. It was slightly ajar, and yet more of the indefatigable brambles could be seen through the holes in its rotten panels. Wild horses could not have stopped us pushing that door open. It squealed and groaned, but by rocking it gently to and fro we eased a gap big enough to squeeze through, back into the impenetrable undergrowth.

It was an unforgettable moment. Close in front of us we could see the finial of a glasshouse gable-end at a crazy angle, like a sinking ship. To our right was the door into another glasshouse. Most of the glass was broken, and what remained was of a curious size and shape, but by peering in we could make out that it was the start of a range that carried on until the all-embracing brambles obscured the view. Cast-iron heating pipes snaked into the distance, tempting us to follow.

Only on turning the rusty door handle did we realize the danger. A small push, and there was the sudden sound of crashing glass. We looked up to see that the whole glasshouse had slipped from the top of the wall and was supported only by the doorframe and the bramble twisting through its cross-members. What little glass that remained was just lying there; the wooden lights which framed it had rotted out years ago. Any sudden movement could have brought it all down, with us underneath. We would have to cut our way around the front of the houses if we were to see what was on the other side. Here we discovered that the door had been the entrance to a matched pair of houses which led into a larger glasshouse with a higher roof and its own entrance from the opposite end. This house seemed to have withstood time's ravages better than the others. Its door gave way with a little screech, and we were in.

The watery morning sun had finally burnt off the clouds, and its dappled light filled the house, giving it a church-like air. A web of brambles choked everything from floor to ceiling. An image of them as nature's stormtroopers came to mind. A garden is a symbol of man's arrogance, perverting nature to human ends; perhaps the brambles were exacting retribution for this vanity by giving a powerful demonstration of the transcience of all things.

Just when I was in danger of becoming seriously depressed by these notions of death and decay I spotted a leaf that didn't look much like a bramble and followed its branch back to the stem. It was a vine, and an old vine at that. Looking up, I could distinguish it weaving in and out of the broken panes along the whole length of the building. There in the midst of all this decay was another, far more powerful symbol—that of regeneration. Perhaps I have an unusually optimistic nature, but I felt hugely excited by this image of resurgence. My eye was drawn to something hanging on the wall: a small pair of rusty scissors, presumably for cutting grapes. How long had they been there?

Who did they belong to? What was their story? What had happened here?

A chap can only take so much of this Indiana Jones stuff, and a pint of bitter beckoned. John and I, wearied by our morning's explorations, decided to go out the easy way, along the farm track. But I knew then that I was enchanted, and that this was more than just a boyish enthusiasm.

ON READING A GARDEN

DOUGLAS CHAMBERS

Douglas Chambers is Professor Emeritus of English at the University of Toronto, a specialist in seventeenth-century literature who has published widely on Milton, Traherne, and Marvell, as well as on social history and, particularly, on the history of gardens. Outside academia, he is best known as the author of *Stonyground: The Making of a Canadian Garden* (1996), excerpted here, a memoir of the one hundred and fifty–acre ancestral farm in Ontario where for twenty years he has been creating a kind of *ferme ornée*, an intricately designed landscape punctuated with pedestals and poetry, where personal attachments are celebrated alongside horticultural history and the land itself. "What I am doing in the gardens of Stonyground," he writes, "speaks back to the landscape what I have learned from it."

. . .

THIS ADDICTION TO GARDENING is ineradicable once it gets hold of you. At this time of the year, it leads you to buy far too many seeds from the nurseries and to devise plans for summer that would employ a whole army of gardeners. I know this, but I do it nonetheless.

Where did it come from, this urge? For most of my life I had no garden, and yet I dreamed of this one, a lost garden of imagined memory to which I might one day find the key. The sources of Stonyground's inspiration are as invisible as the great underground river flowing beneath it that connects Lake Huron and Georgian Bay through unexplored caverns of prehistoric limestone. In his poem "Kubla Khan," Coleridge called the secret river of his inspiration "Alph": the letter "A," the beginning. But that beginning is also in the listening and the attending to what is already there, waiting to speak. And so much of that attending involves the escape from noise: literal noise, and the babel of fashion, those great curses of our time. The God of the Old Testament asks for stillness; so does the muse of the garden.

No one who arrives in a revved-up Camaro or Trans-Am gets time in my garden, and if they come with the sort of super-hyped car stereo that can be heard a quarter of a mile away, their stay is even briefer. I spent (and spend) a lot of my time planting trees to shut out that sort of gratuitous clamour, and I think fondly of that French chain of hotels, the "hôtels du silence" where no radios or TVs are permitted, and cars have to be parked five hundred feet away.

"Why do you not have a cell phone with you when you're working?" ask people who cannot imagine ever being disconnected from an electronic nanny. Nor do they understand that one of the great joys of gardening is to escape from the cyber-gabble that eats up most of our lives: voice-mail, E-mail, all of it the chain-mail of an electronic culture that prevents us from really seeing and hearing. Gardens cannot be made to the sound of music either—any kind of music. They require concentration and, in the process, the total gift of the self to what is there to be discovered.

A true garden is never apart from its landscape. It arises from it like Eve from Adam's rib; it makes love to the fields in the language of botany. What I am doing in the gardens of Stonyground speaks back to the landscape what I have learned from it. Somewhere there is my father naming the spring wild flowers on walks in the woods, an uncle's mysterious cabinet of wild seeds, my grandmother in her large straw hat among the flowers in her border, the last white pine preserved by a great-uncle from a speculating lumberman.

And over and around these things are stories, as indelibly a part of the place as the sweet rocket and money plant (or "silver dollar," as it's called here) that still run riot in the neglected corners in springtime. These are the stories that my great-aunts told about this place, their place, and about the family history that preceded it: stories of resistance and of making a new life. Told over and over again, though never exactly the same, they are as much a part of the fabric of this place as the maples planted by my great-grandmother that overshadow the house.

But I have also been taught how to appreciate these stories and to decode their real meanings by some of the great gardeners and garden writers of the past. The history of this garden is part of the history of gardens generally, and I needed to learn that language in order to understand the meanings of my garden. And that is why Stonyground is also a sort of history of the history of gardens, a collection of references and symbols that celebrates how this knowledge has been discovered and passed down.

One of these horticultural forbears, from whom I learned to "read" my own garden, was the eminent twentieth-century English gardener Gertrude Jekyll. She found the inspiration for her garden borders in the cottage gardens of Surrey: gardens that agricultural labourers had made from the flowers in the lanes and hedgerows where they worked. And so she took the quiet beauties of these ordinary lyric places and gave them epic settings.

In a culture that prized the garish horrors of marigolds in carpet-bed plantings, what she did was as startling to her contemporaries as it is to North American tourists now. For here, in the famous gardens of Sissinghurst and Great Dixter and Hidcote that are indebted to her influence, are the ordinary weeds of our countryside: goldenrod and Joe-Pye weed and black-eyed Susan. Indeed, these and the cardinal flower and blue lobelia and viper's bugloss (that the locals here call "blue devil") were the very plants collected in the 1690s by the great horticultural pioneer Mary Capel Somerset, Duchess of Beaufort, and propagated in her gardens at Badminton.

Dazzled by the polyester vulgarity of shocking-pink impatiens and red salvia and "fire-chief" petunias, we miss the simple elegance of these roadside beauties. "Now," said a scandalized local visitor to Stonyground, confronting some Queen Anne's lace in the rose bed, "if that were in my garden, I'd have had it out." Behind me, in my memory, I could hear the ghostly cackle of my great-Aunt Ella laughing about the gentrified affectations of her city sister when she visited here. "All week she worked, pulling up those pink flowers in the border. 'Now you get the rest of that sweet rocket out of there,' she said to me." Aunt Ella laughs. "It's coming up there again now as thick as hairs on a dog's back." These stories are also the garden's sources, the voices of its muse.

But its source was in Eden too, Milton's Eden, the Eden of *Paradise Lost.* Where had Milton's ideas for a paradisal garden come from? I had wondered, early in the 1970s, when I began to work on a book on that subject. The flowery arbours and wooded alleys looked Italian, but the cattle and tedded grass were out of the English agriculture of the seventeenth century. Milton's Adam and Eve live in paradise, but they work in a garden that is also a farm. And out of such a vision came the English landscape garden. Why could I not reimagine such a thing here? And so it began.

THE FIRST GARDEN

MIDGE ELLIS KEEBLE

M idge Ellis Keeble began her career as an actress, became a broadcaster, then a teacher, but through it all she was a gardener. For more than half a century and across six Canadian gardens that ranged in quality of light, soil, and weather from the desperate to the divine, Keeble dug and grew and gleaned. As she points out in the introduction to her delightful memoir, *Tottering in My Garden* (1989), this is neither a ladylike nor a leisurely pursuit. Instead, the gardener is held in thrall by houses that throw too much shade, animals that gambol through the beds, windstorms that whip up out of nowhere. "A little perfection some of the time is what we settle for and, for most of us, this spells content."

. . .

THE GREAT GARDENS of the world were the result of conscious intent on the part of both owner and architect. There are also gardens of less grandeur where the owner has known what he was about before he started. But in most instances, the average householder, particularly in North America, decides to have a garden because he has a yard. He has a yard because he has a house. And he has a house because he got married and then had children and they needed more room, so he bought a house with a yard. Now he has to do something about the yard.

When our first two children were very much present and a third was about to arrive, Gordon and I chose a small house in a small town north of Toronto. The inevitable yard, securely fenced, was intended to be no more than an out-sized playpen. The builder had tossed grass seed around and about, front and back, and this had grown thick and green, which should have told us something if we had known anything at all. But neither of us had planted a seed in our lives. We bought a fourteen-dollar lawnmower at Eaton's and Gordon cut the grass.

The playpen remained a playpen for about two years and then Jon was six, in first grade, and not to be hemmed in. Elizabeth shinnied up the fence and then up the nearest tree. David, a logical type, found something to stand on, unlocked the gate and walked out.

The yard was empty.

The day stays vividly in my mind. It was April so it could have been raining, but it wasn't. It was Monday so my neighbour Alice could have been washing her husband's socks, but she was out enjoying the sunshine. *House Beautiful* could have minded its own affairs and stuck to house interiors. I don't know who was responsible for the shovel.

It's all too late now and I can't turn back the clock. The day was bright with a warm sun. *House Beautiful* arrived and

for reasons best known to itself had taken a flyer in the direction of gardening. It was a one-page article explaining how "You
Can Grow Enough Food for Four" in a fifteen-by-twenty-foot
plot. The full-page colour picture showed lush green pea pods
hanging from a neat trellis, chunky lettuces all in a row, tomato
plants heavy with fruit, and beside all this a charming young
woman, straight from the model agency, not a hair out of place,
lightly holding a rake and smiling.

Magazine in hand, I strolled out into the sunshine. Alice
was out in her yard, and leaning casually against the fence was
a shovel. Alice said she didn't own it. I didn't own it either, but
I picked it up and pointed it at the ground, and it slid down into
deep, dark, moist, rich earth that turned over easy as breathing.
Peering into the hole, I could see more of the same below. Alice
came over to see what I was doing and picked up the magazine.
Look at all that food! Think of the money we'd save! We read
the directions carefully together and decided we had better follow them word for word. We were advised that, to grow this
amount of produce in so small a space it would be necessary to
thoroughly enrich the soil.

We were standing on the site of an old cow barn and about
three feet of pure compost, but to us it was only dirt and
you grew things in it. So we enriched it. We turned over two
fifteen-by-twenty-foot plots. It was a breeze. We added cow
manure, bone meal, blood meal, wood ashes and then topped
it all off with a load of topsoil. Between us we must have spent a
month's grocery money on rakes, hoes, weeders and seeds. Still

following directions, we planted the seeds closely. The result was staggering.

My two-year-old, intrigued with all the activity, collected all the leftover seeds, stirred them vigorously in a cup, spread them over a square yard by the back door and then jumped up and down on them. This was the first example of high, wide, intensive planting I had ever seen and was so successful I really should have paid more attention.

All three of us were now inundated with peas, carrots, beans, beets and tomatoes. In this small country town, every family had a garden, and immediately neighbours were delighted to hand over their surplus produce to us. Now they politely turned the other way, hoping we would not try to unload our bounty on them. What to do with it? We had no freezers and the only things we knew how to put up safely were the tomatoes. Gradually our basements were chock full of crimson jars; and the window-sills, inside and out, were lined with large, green globes turning relentlessly red. I knew Alice had come to the end of the line when I came out one morning to find her throwing rocks at her garden and yelling, "Stop!"

And though we laughed, it wasn't entirely a joke. We were both weary of spending what should have been the long, lazy days of summer boiling up more jars of tomato chutney, which would never be eaten. That evening her husband quietly turned the vegetable garden under and put down grass. He had had it with beans, he said, and Alice was happily broiling a steak.

My husband too had gone shopping, but not for a steak. He had bought me a present, the best book on gardening he could find, a gold medal in honour of my green thumb. In my opinion, there's no such thing as a green thumb. Either you know what you're doing or you don't. As innocent as two Eves, Alice and I had been working in a gardener's paradise. Apart from the deep compost, we were on top of a hill with superlative drainage, in full sun and facing south. The weather had alternated between misty rains and sunny days—a fool's paradise where one could do no wrong. Alice was no fool. She had taken to sitting in a lawn chair and watching proceedings from there.

For me, there was no escape. The book of knowledge had arrived and the least I could do was glance through it. This was *The Complete Book of Garden Magic* by Roy E. Biles, published in Chicago by the J.G. Ferguson Publishing Co. It is now out of print, but it would be worth your while to search through second-hand book stores or your public library. I can't think of a more basic, encyclopaedic mine of information for the beginner.

The magic in what Mr. Biles believes is digging, sometimes double digging. He is the advocate of the deep, wide hole; and in case you should be tempted to modify a little, he tells you exactly how deep and how wide in feet and inches. If there is something you don't know, he soon makes sure that you do know. Innocence is destroyed.

Dipping gingerly into the pages, I found a chapter on bugs. Bugs? What bugs? Skipping that, I found a picture of hybrid tea roses. On page 123 there was a cross-section drawing of how to prepare a rose bed. Instruction: excavate the entire bed to a depth of two feet. I shall pause here to allow time for reeling around and protesting...

I managed to make one mistake with this garden. I let it persuade me that I was a gardener.

On the other hand, every garden teaches you something. Though the flowers and vegetables have faded from memory, I remember the earth. I can feel it warm and rich in my hands like soft bread crumbs. It was dark, deep brown, not black, and it smelled good. Over the years I have kept trying to find it again.

RIGHT GOOD GROUND

PLINY THE ELDER

Gaius Plinius Secundus (23/24–79 AD) was born in northern Italy and came to Rome at an early age to practice law. He did military service in Germany, spent time in Africa, Judea, and Syria as a prefect, and eventually died during the eruption of Vesuvius that overwhelmed Pompeii. Of his seven books, only *Historiae Naturalis (Natural History in Thirty-seven Books)* survives. Brilliantly translated into English in 1601 by Philemon Holland, *Natural History* discourses on everything from the shape of the earth to the habits of the Mouthless Men who subsist on the fragrance of flowers and fruit. From Pliny's garden of fascinating facts and fancy comes this note on the smell of good soil, to which seasoned gardeners respond today as surely as they did two thousand years ago.

. . .

WELL, TO SPEAKE at a word, surely that ground is best of all other, which hath an aromaticall smell and tast with it. Now if we list moreover to be better instructed, what kind of savour and odour that should be, which we would so gladly find in the earth; we may oftentimes meet with that sent [scent], even when she is not stirred with the plough, but lieth stil and quiet, namely, a little before the sun-setting, especially where a rainbow seemeth to settle and pitch her tips in the Horizon: also, when after some long and continuall drought, it beginneth to rain; for then being wet and drenched therwith, the earth will send up a vapor and exhalation (conceived from the Sun) so heavenly and divine, as no perfume (how pleasant soever it be) is comparable to it.

This smell there must be in it when you ere it up with the plough: which if a man find once, he may be assured it is a right good ground; for this rule never faileth: so as (to say a truth) it is the very smel and nothing els, that will judge best of the earth: and such commonly are new broken grounds, where old woods were lately stocked up: for all men by a generall consent, do commend such for excellent.

Moreover, the same ground for bearing is held to be far better, whensoever it hath rested between, and either lain ley or fallow; whereas for vineyards it is clean contrary: and therefore the more care and diligence is to be emploied in chusing such ground, least wee approove and verifie their opinion, who say, That the soile of all Italie is alreadie out of heart and weary with bearing fruit. This is certaine, that both there and elsewhere, the constitution of the aire and weather, both giveth and taketh away the opportunitie of good husbandrie, that a man cannot otherwhiles do what he would: for some kind of grounds there is so fat and ready to resolve into mire and dirt, that it is impossible to plough them and make good worke, after a shower of raine. Contrariwise, in Byzacium a territory of Africke, it is far otherwise: for there is not a better and more fruitfull piece of ground lieth without dore than it is, yeelding ordinarily 150 fold; let the season be dry, the strongest teeme of oxen that is, cannot plough it: fall there once a good ground shower, one poore asse, with the help of a silly old woman drawing the ploughshare at another side, will be able to go round away with it, as I my selfe have seen many a time and often.

And whereas some great husbands there be, that teach us to inrich and mend one ground with another, to wit, by spreading fat earth upon a lean and hungry soile; and likewise by casting drie, light, and thirstie mould, upon that which is moist and overfat; it is a meere follie and wastfull expence both of time and travaile: for what fruit can he ever looke to reape from such a mingle mangle of ground?

Translation by Philemon Holland

PREPARATIONS

KAREL CAPEK

One of the most influential Czech writers of the twentieth century, Karel Capek (1890–1938) is best remembered for his play *R.U.R.* (*Rossum's Universal Robots*), in which his brother and collaborator, Josef, coined the word "robot" from the Czech word for forced labor. Karel was famous for his Friday garden parties for Czech patriots; in 1929, he took time out from writing his darkly comic fiction to produce a singular collection of essays that follow the calendar year through that same backyard garden in Prague. Illustrated with Josef's whimsical drawings, *The Gardener's Year* survived as a timeless classic to be reissued in 1984. Karel stopped eating when the West abandoned his country to Hitler and died of pneumonia shortly before World War II began. Josef died in 1945 in Bergen-Belsen.

• • •

WHY TRY to conceal it? Already there are unmistakable signs that Nature is lying down to her winter sleep. Leaf after leaf drops from my birches with a beautiful and sad motion; when

they have flowered the plants withdraw again into the earth;
after they have grown and blossomed they leave behind only
a naked stalk or a moist stump, a crabbed brush or a withered
stem; and the soil itself smells sadly of decay. Why try to conceal the fact? It is finished for this year. Chrysanthemum, don't
deceive yourself about the fullness of life; little white potentilla,
don't confuse this last sunshine with the exuberant brilliance of
March. It is of no use to complain, children, the parade is over;
lie down gently to your winter sleep.

But no! But no! What do you mean? Don't say that! What
kind of a sleep is this? Every year we say that Nature lies down
to her winter sleep; but we have not yet looked closely at this
sleep; or, to be more precise, we have not looked at it yet from
below. You must turn things upside down to know them better;
Nature must be turned upside down so that you can look into it;
turn her roots up. Good Lord, is this sleep? You call this a rest?
It would be better to say that vegetation had ceased to grow
upwards, because it has no time for it now; for it has turned its
sleeves up and grows downwards, it spits in its hands and digs
itself into the ground. Look, this pale thing here in the earth is a
mass of new roots; look how far they push; heave-ho! heave-ho!
Can't you hear how the earth is cracking under this enraged and
collective charge? I beg to announce, general, that the storm
troops of roots have won their way into the enemies' ground;
the scouts of phloxes came into contact with the advance patrols
of the campanulas. All right; let them dig themselves in in the
conquered territory; the objectives have been gained.

And these fat, white, and frail things here are new germs and shoots. See how many there are; how bushy you have recently become, faded and withered perennial, how self-confident you are, how overflowing with life! You call this sleep? May the devil take leaves and flowers! Don't be sentimental! Here below, here underground, is the real work, here, here, and here new stems are growing; from here to there, within these November limits, the life of March will spring up; here underground the great programme of spring is laid down. The time to rest has not come yet; look, here is the plan of the building, here the foundations are dug and the drains are laid; and we shall sap further yet, before the soil hardens in the frost. Let spring build green vaults over the pioneer work of the autumn. We underground forces have done our duty.

A hard and fat bud underground, a swelling on the top of a bulb, a strange outgrowth under the heels of dry foliage, a bomb out of which a spring flower will burst. We say that spring is the time for germination; really the time for germination is autumn. While we only look at Nature it is fairly true to say that autumn is the end of the year; but still more true it is that autumn is the beginning of the year. It is a popular opinion that in autumn leaves fall off, and I really cannot deny it; I assert only that in a certain deeper sense autumn is the time when in fact the leaves bud. Leaves wither because winter begins; but they also wither because spring is already beginning, because new buds are being made, as tiny as percussion caps out of which the spring will crack. It is an optical illusion that trees and bushes are naked

in autumn; they are, in fact, sprinkled over with everything that
will unpack and unroll in spring. It is only an optical illusion that
my flowers die in autumn; for in reality they are born. We say
that Nature rests, yet she is working like mad. She has only shut
up shop and pulled the shutters down; but behind them she is
unpacking new goods, and the shelves are becoming so full that
they bend under the load. This is the real spring; what is not
done now will not be done in April. The future is not in front
of us, for it is here already in the shape of a germ; already it is
with us; and what is not with us will not be even in the future.
We don't see germs because they are under the earth; we don't
know the future because it is within us. Sometimes we seem to
smell of decay, encumbered by the faded remains of the past; but
if only we could see how many fat and white shoots are pushing forward in the old tilled soil, which is called the present day;
how many seeds germinate in secret; how many old plants draw
themselves together and concentrate into a living bud, which
one day will burst into flowering life—if we could only see that
secret swarming of the future within us, we should say that our
melancholy and distrust is silly and absurd, and that the best
thing of all is to be a living man—that is, a man who grows.

Translation by M. and R. Weatherall

A GERMAN GARDEN

ELIZABETH VON ARNIM

B orn Marie Annette Beauchamp, Elizabeth von Arnim (1866–1941) left
Australia for a British education. While traveling in Italy, she met and
married a German count, fondly called the Man of Wrath in her first novel,
Elizabeth and her German Garden (1898), which she published anonymously.
Inspired by the derelict garden surrounding the schloss where they lived, the
book was a huge success. She published twenty-one more, first as "the author
of *Elizabeth and Her German Garden*," then simply as "Elizabeth." After the
count's death, von Arnim built a chateau in Switzerland where she wrote
and entertained literati such as H. G. Wells, E. M. Forster, and her cousin,
Katherine Mansfield. Her saucy independence as a gardener in her first
book, excerpted here, has perennial appeal for feminists and gardeners alike.

. . .

I KNEW NOTHING whatever last year about gardening and this
year know very little more, but I have dawnings of what may be
done, and have at least made one great stride—from Ipomoea to
tea-roses.

The garden was an absolute wilderness. It is all round the house, but the principal part is on the south side and has evidently always been so. The south front is one-storied, a long series of rooms opening one into the other, and the walls are covered with virginia creeper. There is a little verandah in the middle, leading by a flight of rickety wooden steps down into what seems to have been the only spot in the whole place that was ever cared for. This is a semicircle cut into the lawn and edged with privet, and in this semicircle are eleven beds of different sizes bordered with box and arranged round a sun-dial, and the sun-dial is very venerable and moss-grown, and greatly beloved by me. These beds were the only sign of any attempt at gardening to be seen (except a solitary crocus that came up all by itself each spring in the grass, not because it wanted to, but because it could not help it), and these I had sown with ipomoea, the whole eleven, having found a German gardening book, according to which ipomoea in vast quantities was the one thing needful to turn the most hideous desert into a paradise. Nothing else in that book was recommended with anything like the same warmth, and being entirely ignorant of the quantity of seed necessary, I bought ten pounds of it and had it sown not only in the eleven beds but round nearly every tree, and then waited in great agitation for the promised paradise to appear. It did not, and I learned my first lesson.

Luckily I had sown two great patches of sweet-peas which made me very happy all the summer, and then there were some sunflowers and a few hollyhocks under the south windows, with

Madonna lilies in between. But the lilies, after being transplanted, disappeared to my great dismay, for who was I to know
it was the way of lilies? And the hollyhocks turned out to be
rather ugly colours, so that my first summer was decorated and
beautified solely by sweet-peas.

At present we are only just beginning to breathe after the
bustle of getting new beds and borders and paths made in time
for this summer. The eleven beds round the sun-dial are filled
with roses, but I see already that I have made mistakes with
some. As I have not a living soul with whom to hold commu-
nion on this or indeed on any matter, my only way of learning
is by making mistakes. All eleven were to have been carpeted
with purple pansies, but finding that I had not enough and that
nobody had any to sell me, only six have got their pansies, the
others being sown with dwarf mignonette. Two of the eleven
are filled with Marie van Houtte roses, two with Viscountess
Folkestone, two with Laurette Messimy, one with Souvenir de
la Malmaison, one with Adam and Devoniensis, two with Persian Yellow and Bicolor, and one big bed behind the sun-dial
with three sorts of red roses (seventy-two in all), Duke of Teck,
Cheshunt Scarlett, and Prefet de Limburg. This bed is, I am sure,
a mistake, and several of the others are, I think, but of course I
must wait and see, being such an ignorant person. Then I have
had two long beds made in the grass on either side of the semicircle, each sown with mignonette, and one filled with Marie
van Houtte, and the other with Jules Finger and the Bride; and
in a warm corner under the drawing-room windows is a bed of

Madame Lambard, Madame de Watteville, and Comtesse Riza du Parc; while farther down the garden, sheltered on the north and west by a group of beeches and lilacs, is another large bed, containing Rubens, Madame Joseph Schwartz, and the Hon. Edith Gifford. All these roses are dwarf; I have only two standards in the whole garden, two Madame George Bruants, and they look like broomsticks. How I long for the day when the tea-roses open their buds! Never did I look forward so intensely to anything; and every day I go the rounds, admiring what the dear little things have achieved in the twenty-four hours in the way of new leaf or increase of lovely red shoot.

The hollyhocks and lilies (now flourishing) are still under the south windows in a narrow border on the top of a grass slope, at the foot of which I have sown two long borders of sweet-peas facing the rose beds, so that my roses may have something almost as sweet as themselves to look at until the autumn, when everything is to make place for more tea-roses. The path leading away from this semicircle down the garden is bordered with China roses, white and pink, with here and there a Persian Yellow. I wish now I had put tea-roses there, and I have misgivings as to the effect of the Persian Yellows among the Chinas, for the Chinas are such wee little baby things, and the Persian Yellows look as though they intended to be big bushes.

There is not a creature in all this part of the world who could in the least understand with what heart-beatings I am looking forward to the flowering of these roses, and not a German gardening book that does not relegate all tea-roses to hot-houses, imprisoning them for life, and depriving them for ever of the breath of God. It was no doubt because I was so ignorant that I rushed in where Teutonic angels fear to tread and made my tea-roses face a northern winter; but they did face it under fir branches and leaves, and not one has suffered, and they are looking today as happy and as determined to enjoy themselves as any roses, I am sure, in Europe.

CAPTIVE GARDENS

COLETTE

The name Sidonie Gabrielle Claudine Colette Gauthier-Villars de Jouvanel Goudeket may not be familiar, but as Colette (1873–1954), this woman is one of the most famous in French letters. Author of more than fifty novels and scores of short stories, Colette grew up in her mother's gardens at Saint-Saveur-en-Puisaye, where plants were her earliest companions. Her first works, the Claudine novels, were published under her husband's pseudonym, Willy. After they divorced, she became a music-hall dancer, political writer, fashion critic, cooking columnist, and eventually a respected novelist under her own name, most famously for *Gigi* (1945). She was the second woman in history to be made a grand officer of the Legion of Honor, and when she died, her mime teacher, George Wague, had a thousand lilies heaped upon her grave. Although never a garden writer, she uses gardens lavishly as fictional motifs and occasionally in her essays turns on them her incisive, defiant intellect, as in this excerpt from *Journey for Myself: Selfish Memories.*

TWO MONTHS AGO, my neighbour was jealous of my golde-
chain laburnum, then of my wisteria, already brawny despite
its youth, leaping from wall to lime-tree, from lime-tree to
the climbing roses, its serpentine limbs dripping with mauve
clusters, heavy with scent. But at the same time, I was glanc-
ing enviously at his double-flowering cherries, and tell me, how
will I compete, come July, with his geraniums? Their red velvet
shows off at high noon as an ineffable violet, mysteriously pro-
voked by the vertical light... Patience! Just wait until he sees
my purple sages in October and November.

Without putting it off that long, he can always cast an apprais-
ing eye on these ambitious crossed sticks hung with masses of
roses, their heads lolling like drunkards', that I honour with the
name "rose garden." The shade flowers I have abandoned to my
other neighbour: the clematis that is more blue than purple, the
lily of the valley, the begonias that are blown after just an hour
in the sun. An old garden nearby harbours a giant Rose of Sharon, in whose service all other vegetation must be sacrificed, for
it is lovely, ancient, indefatigable, and it wears a constant blaze
of blooms that show pink on opening, mauve as they pass their
prime. A red hawthorn, that glory of a Breton spring, glows a
little further away, and a shrubby vine, its vertical lawn trained
in a mosaic up one side of a small mansion, soothes the bucolic
yearnings of a man from Auteuil whose land is but the width
and breadth of an orange-tree planter.

How much longer can such good-natured rivalry call old
folks and sensible children to the threshold of these captive

gardens, brandishing their rakes and hoes, clicking the curved beaks of secateurs, the gardener's perfume of manure and of mown grass in the air? How much longer can it preserve Paris from that cubed sadness, the quadrangular shadows cast by highrises? Every month, in the sixteenth District, an avenue of lime-trees falls, a graceful hedge of euonymous, a venerable arbor rounded to the curve of the crinoline.

Within the past six months, there has risen on the leafy boulevard in front of my house, a block of rental apartments as hideously shaped and showy as a new buck tooth. For a hundred years, a delightful dwelling lay content in the middle of its garden like a hen on her nest of straw; now it is flanked by seven storeys, its right to the sun, its scarab-coloured mornings, its sweet, glowing eventides lost forever. It stands mute, frozen like an extinct planet, wearing its own black shade of mourning.

Nothing can save our captive gardens except the wealth of foreigners. A billionaire from far away develops a passion for a mansion surrounded with gardens in the old quarter. So he buys it and gives it a facelift. He says: "I'd like another two or three like this" to complete his grand vision; and then, he explains: "It's for tennis." We must, in all fairness, admit that from time to time he exhibits a scorn for tennis and bows to all that speaks of France's past. Thanks to him, on a smoothly levelled, regal landscape, Gothic village churches, moved stone by stone like jigsaw puzzles, confront Basque terraces, a faithful reproduction of a Norman orchard, the courtyards of southern France hedged with low, funereal boxwoods, some Breton thatch-cottages, all in the interest of a theatre of the antique. A collection gathered in somewhat unschooled taste, but one which touches those of us provincials imprisoned in Paris, and we shrink from it, we who tremble at the fall of a lilac or the limbing of a chestnut, we who live within a tide of construction that eats into the ever-diminishing Bois, we who fervently defend our narrow strips of green. We sing the praises of what yet remains, but we sing in a melancholy key. Boylesve recalls a garden laid waste. Abel Hermant, though still in possession of his, weeps at the solemn unfolding of spring beneath his balcony, two steps from the Madeleine Church.

The duchess of Sforza raises Morère strawberries between the pillars of a balcony on Henri-Martin and Philippe Berthelot struggles to ripen cherries on the trees he transplanted to the boulevard Montparnasse. Look, on the Saint-Michel quay, a garden built on a roof! On Jacob Street, de Gourmont's lover, the "Amazon," has given up trying to force blooms on the ground floor, where the sun no longer penetrates. But the sparse grass, bent to its knees in supplication to the shade, is sufficient for the night-prowling cat and the barn owl that perches in a dead tree slung with a shred of ivy, like a metaphor from some book. It takes only a little vine, a pale leaf on the wall, to soothe the eye that flits from a blank page to window pane, from window to blank page.

One day, a door on a nondescript street opened and showed me a kind of paradise, profoundly provincial, adorned with ancient weeping ashes, magnolias, stone pots, dozing cats, even espaliered apple trees, planted in the traditional way around the edge of the lawn . . . Espaliered apple trees. O pastoral Parisiens, wavers of banners of lilies in May, gatherers of lilacs, you who dote upon a tuft of grass and a snow-drop, won't you preserve the last rustic secrets of Paris? Those sweetly trained apple trees . . .

Translation by Merilyn Simonds

BLITZ FLOWERS

LEWIS GANNETT

Lewis Gannett (1891–1966) was a prolific American journalist and author. Active in leftwing politics through the Hands Off China Committee (1927) and the All-America Anti-Imperialist League (1928), he wrote on foreign affairs for *The Nation*, then produced a daily book review column for the *New York Herald Tribune*, but it is as a garden writer that he found his place in literature. As well as scores of newspaper pieces on his country garden, he produced three books, including *Cream Hill: Discoveries of a Weekend Countryman* (1949). "Each spring," he wrote, "a gardening instinct, sure as the sap rising in the trees, stirs within us. We look about and decide to tame another little bit of ground." This piece from the *Tribune* celebrates Nature's accidental wartime gardens.

. . .

LONDON, JULY 25 [1944]. London, paradoxically, is the gayest where she has been most blitzed. The wound made this summer by flying bombs are, of course, still raw and bare, but cellars and courts shattered into rubble by the German raids of

1940–41 have been taken over by an army of weeds which have turned them into wild gardens, sometimes as gay as any tilled by human hands.

There is the brilliant rose-purple plant that Londoners call rose-bay willow herb. Americans call it fireweed because it blazes wherever a forest fire has raged. It will not grow in the shade, but there is little shade as yet in the London ruins. It likes potash, and the ruins are full of wood ash. It sweeps across this pockmarked city and turns what might have been scars into flaming beauty. You see it everywhere—great meadows of it in Lambeth, where solid tracts were blitzed; waves of it about St. Paul's. Behind Westminster Abbey bits of it are high up where second-story fireplaces still cling to the hanging walls.

The fireweed plant gives the characteristic rose-purple and green color tone to what look like vacant lots all over London—the blitz sites.

London has done a neat job of ordering and inclosing these ruined patches. Dangerous walls have been tumbled down, rubble and bricks heaped and piled, and neat four-foot brick walls today guard the passer-by on the pavement from the cellar holes. Some of these holes have been sealed in and filled as temporary reservoirs, and the image of clumps of fireweed reflected in the water gives added beauty to the picture.

Few of the old ruins are bare. Plant life creeps in almost at once. Only two years after the big blitz of 1940–41, the present director of the Royal Botanical Garden at Kew, Professor E.J. Salisbury, has identified ninety-five species of plants, not counting mosses and fungi growing in the bomb sites. He also eliminated from his count the species found in areas which had formerly been gardens. He counted only plant immigrants into London since the blitz.

Contrasting with the rose-purple of the fireweed are everywhere fiery yellow patches of groundsel, or ragwort, a busy plant with chrysanthemum-like leaves and golden daisy-like blossoms. Three species are abundant in the ruins. The least conspicuous common groundsel is an old resident of England, but the most striking of the three, curiously, is a native of Sicily, at home among the volcanic ashes of Mount Etna. This gay flower was introduced into the botanical gardens at Oxford in 1794 and in England is called the Oxford Ragwort. Its present wild abundance dates from the blitz.

Most of the weeds and wild flowers of the blitz sites are familiar to Americans: red and white clover, musk mallow, evening primrose, chamomile, white and purple-flowering nightshade, wild lettuce, sow thistle, Canada thistle, yellow rocket, hedge mustard, dandelion, knotweed, the various docks, lambs quarters (better known as pigweed), the coarse plant that Americans call horseweed, but in London is known as the Canadian fleabane; the daisy-like pest which Litchfield County, Conn., calls Germanweed, but which the erudite Londers, generally mispronouncing its Latin name, call "gallant soldiers." And the rank, rounded leaves of the common coltsfoot, which in early spring puts up dandelion-like flowers, are part of the picture of almost every blitz site.

The tree of heaven, the Ailanthus, which some of us call the Manhattan back-yard tree and which Betty Smith made famous in "A Tree Grows in Brooklyn," is already beginning to over-shadow the wild flowers in some blitz cellars. But the most common tree to start growing in the ruins is the Goat Willow. There are also incipient poplars and sycamores, presumably seeded from the green squares that dot old London.

A few flowers known to Americans as garden plants are frequently part of the wild gardens in the cellars of London, notably poppies, calendula, larkspur, candytuft and hollyhock, all of which are common sights about Holborn and in the great devastated tacts behind St. Paul's.

Here and there among brick piles in this moist climate of London, ferns have sprung up—sometimes the handsome male fern, which looks at a distance like the spinulose ferns our florists pack with roses, but more often the common bracken. Both grow in the churchyard of St. James's, in Piccadilly, behind Charing Cross station and at Amen Corner. In some cellars behind St. Paul's, bracken is beginning to form miniature bracken heaths.

The botanists say that the most abundant plants on the bomb sites are those with parachute attachments for their seeds. The weedlike yarrow, common beside the well traveled paths on the embankments, is seldom seen in the ruins. Its seeds are usually carried in mud attached to boots or tires, and neither boots nor tires climb down into London's cellar ruins. The most abundant blitz plants—fireweed, groundsels and horseweed—are all air-distributed. Birds carry some seeds, but birds have little interest in cellar sites until vegetation has established itself there, providing food for them.

Today the blitz sites are untended gardens. In another few years the shade provided by these plant pioneers will doubtless permit new types of plant life to appear, and the reigning wild beauties of today will disappear. But London's ruins are not likely to pass through what the botanists call a normal cycle, for London is full of plans and dreams of new types of houses and gardens to spring up where the Germans have so expensively destroyed the old.

THE PUREST
OF PLEASURES

FRANCIS BACON

Lord Chancellor of England, Francis Bacon (1561–1626) was a contemporary of Shakespeare. A philosopher and writer, he occupied the threshold between medieval and modern thought, producing such works as *Colours of Good and Evil, Advancement of Learning,* and the influential *Novum Organum,* in which he pioneered the notion of empirical science. His literary works include a history of Henry VII and *New Atlantis,* but his reputation as a stylist rests upon his *Essays* (1625), from which this excerpt is taken. Written in a conversational tone, the piece, although instructive, is laced with Bacon's personal taste and his imaginative ideal of the perfect garden. The sort of sweeping enclosed space he recommends can still be seen at Boscobel in Shropshire, the garden where Charles II hid from Cromwell and his troops.

. . .

GOD ALMIGHTY FIRST PLANTED a garden. And indeed, it is the purest of human pleasures; it is the greatest refreshment to the spirits of man, without which buildings and palaces are but

75

gross handiworks. And a man shall ever see that when ages grow to civility and elegancy, men come to build stately, sooner than to garden finely, as if gardening were the greater perfection . . .

For gardens (speaking of those which are indeed prince-like, as we have done of buildings), the contents ought not well to be under thirty acres of ground; and to be divided into three parts: a green in the entrance, a heath or desert in the going forth, and the main garden in the midst, besides alleys on both sides. And I like well, that four acres of ground be assigned to the green, six to the heath, four and four to either side, and twelve to the main garden. The green hath two pleasures: the one, because nothing is more pleasant to the eye than green grass kept finely shorn; the other, because it will give you a fair alley in the midst, by which you may go in front upon a stately hedge, which is to inclose the garden. But, because the alley will be long, and in great heat of the year, or day, you ought not to buy the shade in the garden by going in the sun through the green; therefore you are of either side the green to plant a covert alley, upon carpenter's work about twelve foot in height, by which you may go in shade into the garden.

As for the making of knots, or figures, with divers colored earths, that they may lie under the windows of the house, on that side which the garden stands, they be but toys. You may see as good sights many times in tarts.

The garden is best to be square, encompassed on all the four sides with a stately arched hedge. The arches to be upon pillars of carpenter's work, of some ten foot high and six foot broad, and the spaces between of the same dimension with the breadth of the arch; over the arches let there be an entire hedge of some four foot high, framed also upon carpenter's work; and upon the upper hedge, over every arch, a little turret with a belly, enough to receive a cage of birds; and over every space, between the arches, some other little figure, with broad plates of round colored glass, gilt, for the sun to play upon. But this hedge I intend to be raised upon a bank, not steep, but gently sloped, of some six foot, set all with flowers. Also, I understand, that this square of the garden should not be the whole breadth of the ground, but to leave on either side ground enough for diversity of side alleys, unto which the two covert alleys of the green may deliver you. But there must be no alleys with hedges at either end of this great inclosure: not at the hither end for letting your prospect upon this fair hedge from the green; nor, at the further end, for letting your prospect from the hedge, through the arches, upon the heath.

For the ordering of the ground within the great hedge, I leave it to variety of device; advising, nevertheless, that whatsoever form you cast it into, first it be not too busy or full of work. Wherein I, for my part, do not like images cut out in juniper or other garden stuff—they be for children. Little low hedges, round, like welts, with some pretty pyramids, I like well, and in some places fair columns upon frames of carpenter's work. I would also have the alleys spacious and fair. You may have closer alleys upon the side grounds, but none in the main garden.

I wish also in the very middle a fair mount with three ascents and alleys, enough for four to walk abreast, which I would have to be perfect circles, without any bulwarks or embossments, and the whole mount to be thirty foot high; and some fine banqueting house, with some chimneys neatly cast, and without too much glass.

For fountains, they are a great beauty and refreshment; but pools mar all, and make the garden unwholesome and full of flies and frogs. Fountains I intend to be of two natures—the one that sprinkleth or spouteth water, the other a fair receipt of water, of some thirty or forty foot square, but without fish, or slime, or mud. For the first, the ornaments of images gilt, or of marble, which are in use, do well; but the main matter is, so to convey the water as it never stay, either in the bowls or in the cistern, that the water be never by rest discolored, green, or red, or the like, or gather any mossiness or putrefaction. Besides that, it is to be cleansed every day by the hand. Also some steps up to it and some fine pavement about it, doth well. As for the other kind of fountain, which we may call a bathing pool, it may admit much curiosity and beauty, wherewith we will not trouble ourselves; as that the bottom be finely paved, and with images; the sides likewise, and withal embellished with colored glass, and such things of lustre, encompassed also with fine rails of low statues. But the main point is the same, which we mentioned in the former kind of fountain, which is, that the water be in perpetual motion, fed by a water higher than the pool, and delivered into it by fair spouts, and then discharged away under ground by some equality of bores, that it stay little. And for fine devices, of arching water without spilling, and making it rise in several forms (of feathers, drinking glasses, canopies, and the like), they be pretty things to look on, but nothing to health and sweetness.

For the health, which was the third part of our plot, I wish it to be framed, as much as may be, to a natural wildness. Trees I would have none in it; but some thickets, made only of sweetbriar and honeysuckle, and some wild vine amongst; and the ground set with violets, strawberries, and primroses; for these are sweet, and prosper in the shade; and these to be in the heath, here and there, not in any order. I like also little heaps, in the nature of mole-hills (such as are in wild heaths) to be set, some with wild thyme, some with pinks, some with germander that gives a good flower to the eye; some with periwinkle, some with violets, some with strawberries, some with cowslips, some with daisies, some with red roses, some with *Lilium convallium,* some with sweetwilliams, red, some with bear's-foot, and the like low flowers, being withal sweet and sightly. Part of which heaps to be with standards of little bushes pricked upon their top, and part without. The standards to be roses, juniper, holly, bearberries (but here and there, because of the smell of their blossom), red currants, gooseberries, rosemary, bays, sweetbriar, and such like. But these standards to be kept with cutting, that they grow not out of course.

For the side grounds you are to fill them with variety of alleys, private, to give a full shade, some of them wheresoever the sun be. You are to frame some of them likewise for shelter, that when the wind blows sharp you may walk as in a gallery. And those alleys must be likewise hedged at both ends to keep out the wind, and these closer alleys must be ever finely gravelled, and no grass, because of going wet. In many of these alleys, likewise, you are to set fruit-trees of all sorts, as well upon the walls as in ranges. And this would be generally observed that the borders wherein you plant your fruit-trees be fair and large and low, and not steep, and set with fine flowers, but thin and sparingly, lest they deceive the trees. At the end of both the side grounds I would have a mount of some pretty height, leaving the wall of the enclosure breast high, to look abroad into the fields.

For the main garden I do not deny but there should be some fair alleys, ranged on both sides with fruit-trees and some pretty tufts of fruit-trees, and arbors with seats set in some decent order; but these to be by no means set too thick, but to leave the main garden so as it be not close, but the air open and free. For, as for shade, I would have you rest upon the alleys of the side grounds, there to walk, if you be disposed, in the heat of the year or day, but to make account that the main garden is for the more temperate parts of the year, and in the heat of summer for the morning and the evening, or overcast days.

So I have made a platform of a princely garden, partly by precept, partly by drawing, not a model, but some general lines of it; and in this I have spared for no cost. But it is nothing for great princes that, for the most part taking advice with workmen, with no less cost set their things together, and sometimes add statues and such things for state and magnificence, but nothing to the true pleasure of a garden.

ON SUPPLANTING
RAMPANT NETTLEDOM
WITH A WONDROUS
WATERY REALM

ELIZABETH SMART

Elizabeth Smart (1913–1986) is best remembered for her lyrical novel *By Grand Central Station I Sat Down and Wept* (1945). Initially suppressed in Canada, it is now considered a classic. After supporting herself and her four children with magazine work, Smart retired to a cottage in north Suffolk where she took up literary writing again. As well as five books, she wrote a gardening column for *Harper's Bazaar* and kept multiple diaries, including eleven journals and twenty notebooks devoted to gardening, which are excerpted in *Elizabeth's Garden: Elizabeth Smart on the Art of Gardening* (1989). As passionate about plants as language, she gave her beds such names as the Magic Circle and the Poet's Corner. Here, she describes the creation of a water garden.

. . .

ONE DAY IN the first summer, I was sitting on the terrace in the sun contemplating a sea of nettles stretching away to the boundaries of the Dell, when I thought, "Wouldn't it be lovely to have an oval pond just *there,* cutting out those nettles forever with fish and water lilies and weeping willows instead?" It is the possibility of realizing such godlike ideas that makes gardening so compulsive.

So I said to a kind son who happened to be there at that moment, "Wouldn't it be lovely etc.?"

And he said, "Mmm..."

So I showed him some instigating brochures I happened to have by me (in the early days of gardening you contrive to have indiscriminate brochures arriving by every post). This one had easy step-by-step instructions for instant idyllic results, and he suddenly said, "Why not?" and started digging like a mad thing. Lo and behold, next day there was a pool-shaped oval, 15 feet long by 10 feet wide, 2 feet deep in the middle with the recommended shallower 8 inch ledge around the edges. It was speedy and triumphant while he shovelled out the sand, though when he struck clay and rubbish dumps the going was not so good. But I moved out of earshot and sent away for the requisite giant plastic sheet. We found a local firm willing to sell us a laughably small amount of paving slabs which were duly dumped at the gate, heaved into my son's car and backed up to the pool hole. We draped the plastic over the hole and anchored it with the slabs, and there it was, all ready for water, if far from ready for the nymphs.

The garden hose-pipe didn't reach anywhere near it. So I bought another and joined them together. Now it reached just a maddening two feet from the pond. So I bought *another,* and at last the water started to trickle in. It trickled night and day for two days, taking out the wrinkles in the plastic and getting us all enthusiastic again. Then my next-door farmer knocked on the door and said, "What's up? The cattle have no water." But the pond was full by then so I said: "Sorry, it won't happen again," and was forgiven. Then my son got busy cracking the paving stones and cementing them round while I sent away for a "well-balanced" collection of pool plants and fish and snails: oxygenating plants for the bottom, floating plants to make shade for the fish, five water-lilies (queens of the whole project), and marginal plants for atmosphere. You can buy all these, all carefully sorted out for your particular-sized pool, so everything does its duty and the little watery community exists happily in a practical, Platonic way, everything self-sufficient and mutually beneficial. You could work it out for yourself but for me I felt it safer to begin with the beginner's set.

The plants arrived first and I got into my swimsuit and planted them in their containers and sunk them in their allotted places, bashing on full of faith despite the muddled muddied labels and encroaching darkness. The oxygenating plants, limp bedraggled little objects, seemed interminable, and it was hard to believe that on such could rest the foundations of the state. After the plants are in you have to wait two or three weeks, until they are well settled, before you get the fish and snails. That's why the whole operation is best done in the middle of summer.

My fish at last arrived, but not in the Dell. British Rail telephoned on a Saturday to say they were at Norwich (nineteen miles away) and there were no further road services until next Friday. Would I collect them? How could I? I had no car. Panic! To my relief an insouciant friend in a Jeep drew up to the door and we bounced off pell-mell to the rescue. The fish in their plastic bag were a bit unnerved, but we lowered them gingerly into the water, bag and all, so they could take their time about swimming off into their new home. It was all too much for one or two, who floated to the top and gave up the ghost, but most survived, and the snails settled in in a particularly business-like way.

Then I began collecting large decorative flintstones, to try to hide the inevitable gap between the sky-blue plastic and the raw paving stones, coaxing the marginal plants into nooks and crannies and even resorting to festoons of invasive brooklime to help with the camouflaging. You wouldn't believe how many big flintstones you need to encircle a little pond and how many roll away out of your hands and go plop to the bottom. Interesting work. But so heavy. And very very slow. However, gradually the edges began to look pretty, with water irises, marsh marigolds, water buttercups, water hawthorn, water mint, forget-me-not. By the end of the summer it was beginning to have a lived-in look, with fish darting about and waterlily leaves beginning to spread themselves in their traditional way. In late autumn the floating plants turned a rich mulberry colour, and I began to feel a creeping-on of that smug gardener's feeling, when, suddenly, I heard the hunter's horn. Almost before I could grab the babies and rush inside and bolt the doors, the hounds came sweeping down from all sides of the Dell in terrifying packs followed by galloping scarlet-faced scarlet-clad men on over-excited horses. The whole pack of hounds lolloped straight into the pool, thrashing around, bringing down plants, laboriously-gathered stones and all my watery dreams.

Well, that's gardening. But it was many a long month before I could tell this tale without getting into a fever of impotent rage. Compensation? What's that in gardening? It's the *time*. Another whole year until we're where we were again! Now, two years afterwards, the pool is just beginning to look clothed and natural again, with the waterside plants to bind the flints in place. And any autumn it could happen again, unless I can somehow contrive an impenetrable barrier around the whole of the boundaries of the Dell. And even the quickest quickthorn hedge needs a good five years and Hercules to help with the preparatory digging. And as for man-made fencing, it would cost a fortune to surround the Dell with a thick wire mesh at least eight feet high, and absolutely hound-proof.

Still, each year I go collecting more marsh marigolds and yellow flags, and the water-lilies keep coming up, and the surviving fish have even had babies. You have to abandon pride along with sightly fingernails when you take up gardening.

Last July, just after I had discovered acid soil on the knoll and exultantly moved up all my rhododendrons, there was a gigantic gale and my biggest tree was blown right over, taking away all the necessary overhead protection and leaving the young struggling plants exposed to east and north winds all winter, just when I thought I had them deftly tucked in and all I had to do was wait... and wait... and wait for the years to pass until the flowering spectacle was to be relied upon. They survived. They blossomed. But just in case they find life too hard I have planted masses of foxgloves to march up and down the knoll and give a lavish all's well look and a second line of defence if the worst should happen. You've got to go on. If you don't, chaos is crouching there with the nettles, waiting to take over.

A SNAKE IN
THE GARDEN

EMILY LAWLESS

Irish writer Emily Lawless (1845–1913) wrote nineteen books of fiction,
biography, history, Nature studies, and poetry. Widely read in her time,
she is now mostly remembered for her poems, *With the Wild Geese* (1902)
and *Ireland: A Study* (1885), which can be downloaded as a free ebook at
Project Gutenburg. Her reputation was damaged when William Butler
Yeats accused her of having "an imperfect sympathy with the Celtic nature."
Nevertheless, he included two of her books in his list of the best Irish novels.
A Garden Diary: September 1899–September 1900, excerpted here, straddles
two centuries in tone as well as chronological time, retaining the high-
minded horticultural sentiments characteristic of the 1800s but also allow-
ing the ironic humor and sharp-eyed insights that make her writing highly
entertaining today.

. . .

THE EPIC OF WEEDING has still to be written! It should be
undertaken in no light or frolic vein, but with all the gravity
that the subject demands. What I should wish to see would be

87

either a careful scientific treatise by a competent authority, or, what would perhaps be still better, a great poem, which, like all the highest poetry, would go straight to the very soul of the subject, and leave the votary of it satisfied for ever. To the earnest-minded Weeder, most other occupations seem comparatively subordinate. Blank is that day some portion of which has not been devoted to faithful weeding. Blank is that night in which, as he lays his head upon the pillow, he cannot say to himself that such, or such a piece of ground has been thoroughly cleared, and will not require to be done again—for quite a fortnight!

One disadvantage it certainly has, but then it is one that it shares with all the other higher, and more absorbing pursuits. If inordinately pursued, it tends to grow upon its votary, until everything becomes subsidiary. What was originally a virtue, may thus in time come near to growing into a vice. Of this danger I am myself a proof. There have been moments—not many, nevertheless some—when I have found myself sighing for more weeds to conquer. Worse, I have had the greatest difficulty on more than one occasion to keep myself from pouncing upon my neighbour's perfectly private chickweeds and groundsels, which I have happened to catch sight of across a fence!

I notice in myself, and have observed in others, a lamentable lack of accuracy as regards the proper names of weeds. Even some that I know the best, and hate the hardest, I really cannot put any name to. Now this is not as it should be. Everything, however detestable, has a name of its own, and that name ought to be used. You may not like a man, but that is hardly a reason for calling him "What's-his-name," or "Thingamy." It is true that in the West of Ireland it is regarded as a very unsafe thing to mention any of the more malignant powers by their right names. The *Sidh,* for instance, if spoken of by their proper title, invariable fly at you, and do you a mischief. The only way of avoiding this peril is to use some obscure and roundabout designation, which is not their real name at all. I do not know whether the same mode of reasoning has ever been held to apply to weeds. If so, I cannot say that the plan appears to me to answer. At least I can safely swear that I have never called one of them by its proper botanical name in my life, yet they rush in on us from all sides, and persecute us none the less impishly.

There is one particularly diabolical individual, which has clearly marked this garden as its prey, and marches continually to and fro of it like a roaring lion. What its correct name is I shall in all probability never know, though I have carefully cross-examined several botanical works on the subject. It has narrow fleshy leaves; a mass of roots, constructed of equal parts of pin wire and gutta-percha; the meanest of pinky white flowers, and a smell like sour hay. It is not the leaves, the flowers, the roots, or even the smell, that I so much object to. It is the capacity it possesses of flinging out offshoots of itself to incredible distances, which offshoots no sooner touch ground than they begin to weave a kind of ugly green net over everything within reach, enmeshing it all into as dense a mass of leaves and roots as is the parent plant.

Although I am no nearer extirpating it than I was before, since yesterday I have at least been able to name it, a satisfaction which many a poor Speaker must have been thankful for, especially in an age grown too picked and tender to allow of even the most obdurate obstructor being despatched to either the Tower, or the Block.

It was Cuttle who provided me with that satisfaction, and it is not one of the least of the many debts that I owe him.

"What can be the name of this thing, I wonder, Cuttle?" I said, rising exhausted from an effort to hinder a fresh colony from enmeshing and strangling a line of "Laurette Messimy" which had been recently planted on top of a slope.

"I'm not sure as I can tell you its proper name, ma'am, but about here *we* calls it 'Snaking Tommy.' "

Admirable Cuttle! "Snaking Tommy" of course! The instant I heard it I felt convinced that in that preliminary naming of all plants and animals performed by Adam in the garden of Eden, that, and no other, must have been the name bestowed upon this. It is true some theologian might assure me that there were no weeds in the garden of Eden, but that I think is not particularly likely, because, whether there were weeds in that garden or not, there are certainly no theologians in this one. Moreover, we all know that the snake was there, to everyone's immeasurable discomfort. And if the snake, why not, let me ask, "Snaking Tommy"?

INVASION OF
THE SUMAC

ALLEN LACY

Allen Lacy is one of the most prolific and well-regarded American garden writers of the past fifty years. Professor emeritus of philosophy at Stockton College, he wrote a garden column for the *Wall Street Journal* for five years, then moved to the *New York Times* for seven. Born in Texas, he writes lovingly of his southern New Jersey garden, ranging through philosophy, religion, history, and current events in his exploration of the cultivated world. He published ten books, many of them collections of his columns and occasional writings, including *Farther Afield* (1981), from which this piece is taken. He came to gardening young, "about the same time I was struggling with long division," he recalled in a column titled, "Horticulture is art, science, and sometimes love affair."

. . .

EVER SINCE OUR FIRST parents blew it and then beat it from Eden, every gardener has known that to balance every bright success there's a near-miss or an outright dismal failure.

91

Near-misses and dismal failures come in many shapes and sizes, but the most embarrassing ones take place when we unwittingly invite some very ill-mannered and invasive plant or other into our yards and then watch in horror as it oversteps its bounds, making itself, like Sheridan Whiteside in *The Man Who Came to Dinner*, far too much at home. Most gardeners can list several such mistakes. My own list would take several hours to discuss, if listeners were willing to invest the time in someone else's recital of woes. For starters, there are spiderwort, ox-eye daisy, and old-fashioned tiger lilies, all of which immediately got out of hand, springing up in places where they were neither planted nor wanted. And I may well, in time, regret those pink evening primroses.

I did know better than to put in Equisetum or horsetails. Even though they're genuine botanical curiosities, plants of such evolutionary antiquity as to call forth images of dinosaurs and pterodactyls in the vicinity, they're also such notorious spreaders that one friend of mine who grows them surrounds them with a metal barricade pushed eighteen inches deep into the ground. Bamboo is also nothing to trifle with. I grow it, but in an isolated corner of my garden, where thus far I've kept it under control, partly by cooking and eating those of its shoots which spring up where I don't want them. Spearmint was a calculated risk. It's one of the pushiest herbs on earth—but who could survive the hot afternoons of August without a pitcher of iced tea heavily laced with lots of lemon juice and fresh crushed mint leaves?

It is, alas, extremely simple to name the worst miscalculation I ever made as a gardener. Six or seven years ago, I let the glowing words of a mail-order nursery catalog persuade me that I had desperate need of the shrub *Rhus typhina* "Laciniata"—the staghorn sumac. The catalog seduced me with its talk about the staghorn's subtle and haunting beauty. It also appealed to unimpeachable authority: the Royal Horticultural Society had given it a Garden Merit Award. But perhaps staghorn sumac simply behaves itself better in British gardens.

The staghorn sumac has its merits. It's a fast grower, to understate the matter. Its large, deeply cut, ferny leaves are handsome and bold from midspring into fall. In the winter its nobby, brittle branches are covered with the cinnamon-colored, velvety down that gives it its common name. Nevertheless, after several years of constant battle with it, I'm dogmatically of the opinion that it has no place whatsoever in the home garden and that any nursery that offers it to the public ought to write the words "Let the Buyer Beware" in its catalog before proceeding to celebrate its haunting and subtle beauties. This sumac, like most others in the genus, is an unrelentingly restless wanderer. It doesn't just spread from its center, like some other plants. It does that, but it also sends out underground stems that can meander thirty or forty feet from the mother colony before suddenly springing up in some unexpected spot. And it seems that once you've planted one staghorn on the premises you'll have many more, world without end. Two years after I planted mine, I concluded that it had to go, so I ripped it out—or so I thought.

Its progeny are still with me. I hack them out wherever they pop up. I mutter curses at them, but they thrive on my dislike, proving the point that far from loving Mozart and doting on affectionate remarks addressed to them, plants don't give a fig for our esteem.

Despite some antipathy toward reaching for a chemical solution to every horticultural problem that comes along, in my effort to stem the staghorn tide I've resorted to a herbicide my friends in the nursery business swear by. But however effective it may be in sending chickweed and almost anything else to swift and certain doom, it barely daunts this monster whose far from subtle presence haunts my garden. The shoots die back, but within a month lusty new ones take their place.

But, on reflection, perhaps this plant serves some useful purpose after all. There are days when I want to exult over the fine bloom my clematis is having this season, or the splendid way the new perennial border is coming along, or the excellent growth made by a vitex tree after I removed it from a shaded spot and gave it a place in the sun—days when I want to hog the credit for the beauty of some of the plants I grow. Staghorn sumac keeps me humble.

THE REVOLTING
GARDEN

GERMAINE GREER

Germaine Greer (1939–) became a spokesperson for 1960s feminism
when she published *The Female Eunuch* in 1968. Since then, her
books have charted women's progress through sexuality and fertility (*Sex
and Destiny*, 1984) to menopause (*The Change*, 1991). That this uninhib-
ited six-foot Australian is also a passionate gardener is less well known.
In the 1970s, she moved to London and struggled womanfully to establish an Eden in Notting Hill. The result was *The Revolting Garden* (1979),
which began as a series of columns for the satiric magazine *Private Eye*.
Writing as Rose Blight, Greer hurled herself against horticulture's conven-
tions as vigorously as she railed against traditional male-female relations.
The Revolting Garden is wickedly funny, but also tender and wise. "A garden," she writes, "is the best alternative therapy."

. . .

GROUND COVER

The London garden must be revolting, essentially because the
cultural conditions are so very unfavourable to plant life that

only the dreariest of plants will make do with them and, incidentally, because the last thing the London gardener wants to do is to entice the passing hordes into his domain.

The professional gardener, in hopes to garden all but undetected, favours such irrepressibly boring plants as privet, in particular, *Ligustrum ovalifolium*, which can be relied upon to push its charcoal green leaves doggedly upward through the murk to a height of fifteen feet, meekly parting its grimy limbs to allow dustmen to crash through with their bins, catching up plastic bags and cigarette packets like some egregious scavenging dog.

Its yoke companion is often *Aucuba japonica* or spotted laurel, whose pustular-yellow spattered leaves hang on unabashed when the rest of the garden has withered away under a pile of mattresses, rusting bedsteads, bottles, tin cans and disowned perambulators. If the gardener wishes to act as pander by placing a bough of male blossom on the female plant when it is in bloom, it will bear vivid red fruits which are not, I fear, poisonous.

Another Nip plant, the famous *Fatsia japonica*, also accepts life in conditions of verminous, permanent semi-shade, because its thick stems and leathery leaves are so hideous that it is grateful to be cultivated anywhere.

Labour costs have defeated the public gardeners' penchant for floral bedding schemes. Ground cover is now the rage. Ground cover is the name given to any low, sneaking form of vegetation which will creep, belly-down, through the filth that Londoners call soil, until there is no necessity for weeding or hoeing or, for that matter, gardening. Ivies, loosestrifes and an unlovely thing called *Pachysandra terminalis* are the current favourites.

Lysimachia nummularia or creeping jenny, yellow, prostrate and fast-moving, will cover any old eye-sore in less time than it takes to tell. Mint and balm are popular with inexperienced gardeners, unaware of their fixation upon growing through the roots of other places, leaving unoccupied spaces bare.

Such plantings as these are serviceable and dully repellent; the revolting gardener, who has to look at such vegetation tedium every day, will find little positive excitement in its dutiful dreariness. He will soon aspire to the concoction of something more actively hideous.

SMELLY

One of the most potent weapons in the malevolent gardener's armoury is smell. While others may plant *Anthemis nobilis* or camomile, for the sweet smell given forth by the crushed leaves, he will try *Anthemis cotula* which smells very like hot horse's urine. *Senecio viscosus londinensis* smells of the stale of humbler creatures, ferrets perhaps, which is hardly surprising when one notices that it flourishes around the bases of lampposts. Its relative *Senecio jacobaea* or ragwort, smells less vile, but has the added advantage of being hugely poisonous.

Hypericum calycinum, besides being a grovelling ground cover is, they say, very offensive to dogs. Its relative, *Hypericum hyrcinum*, is also low-growing and has the astonishing virtue of smelling strongly of billy-goat. This remarkable propensity is shared with the spectacular "Lizard" orchid, *Himanthoglossum hyrcinum*, which may grow three feet tall, and has curious unfolding tongues in the flowers. To grow one of these, or even the "Bug" orchid, *Orchis coriophora*, which fills the air with the unmistakable odour of bedbugs, is a tremendous feather in the revolting gardener's cap, for not only do they smell awful they look almost worse, like so many skewers loaded with the entrails of small animals.

It is not easy for the London gardener to grow true garlic, which needs sun and good drainage, but *Allium triquetrum*, a slimier version bred up in the damp shade, will not only keep off bugs, but will discourage the casual human caller as well.

If your garden is really boggy, and the drains occasionally overflow, you may be able to grow the fat, shining skunk cabbage, *Lysichitum*, either the American species, which has a greasy yellow flower, or the Kamchatkan, which is white.

It is very doubtful whether any of these foetid vegetables will make much impression on the masking odour of the London garden, which is an unforgettable blend of tom-cat, grease, burnt rubber and drains. In order to achieve self-defence, the anti-social gardener may find that he has to resort to physical assault.

SELF-DEFENCE

If your garden is all that stands between your domestic hearth and a tourist-junkie-drunk-and-football-fan-infested street, you need to cultivate plants which actually inflict pain upon the unwary interloper. A large holly-bush will defend itself adequately against a toppling drunk or swooning dope-fiend, but, as it is very slow-growing, it may be more rewarding to concentrate upon the more intractable roses.

Rosa felipes "Kiftsgate" is able to strangle full-grown elms. The euphoric freak, about whom she throws her hammock, will indeed die in aromatic pain. If he struggles to break free of her iron caress he may well flay himself to the bone.

The very existence of the "Dunwich Rose" is justified by its astonishing ability to draw blood with its larger spines and to cause weeks of agony with its myriad tiny ones. *Rosa spinosissima* is so extravagantly prickly that it tears all its own leaves off in a high wind.

Most of the really vicious roses only flower as an afterthought, so that passers-by are not actively lured to donate blood and curses. The way to do that is to plant the showier hybrid roses on the far side of a killer rose. Passers-by will willingly run the gamut as soon as the buds begin to blow, and will abuse you roundly when they hurt themselves, all of which is very amusing, unless you loathe leathery hybrid roses and count the game not worth the candle.

Even more dreadful than the dreadful passer-by is the London dog. The combination of a dog and owner is a law unto itself, as I realised when I watched a dog-owner hold open my gate so that her deformed pooch could direct his steaming ammoniac jet right into the smiling faces of my auriculas.

The dog having his eyes and nose close to the ground is relatively vulnerable. *Berberis x stenophylla* has wonderful, long, hidden barbs at dog's eye level. The handsome and useful spurge family is united in its habit of secreting corrosive latex if some fatuous quadruped should bruise its leaves.

ON THE ROOTEDNESS
OF PLANTS

JENNIFER BENNETT

Jennifer Bennett (1949–) was gardening editor of Canada's *Harrowsmith* magazine from its inception until 1991, and hosted the television series *Harrowsmith Country Life*. Her first book, *The Harrowsmith Northern Gardener*, quickly became a cold-climate classic. Of her subsequent seven books, two work unique territory: *Lilies of the Hearth: The Historical Relationship between Women and Plants* (1991) and *Our Gardens, Ourselves: Reflections on an Ancient Art* (1994), excerpted here. Bennett has since become a noted choral director and composer, developing a musical sensibility that was apparent in her early regard for her garden. "What an incredible thing it was," she writes in *Our Gardens, Ourselves*, "this interplay of light and air, water, earth, and plants, this chorus of many parts, all in a shifting counterpoint harmony."

. . .

WHY CAN'T PLANTS WALK? It sounds like a silly question. But given the extravagant possibilities of evolution, why *would* anything end up stuck in one place, subject to every whim of weather and climate, unable to run from fires or chain saws or browsing deer or children making bouquets? Why no legs, fins, wings for independent motion?

The rootedness of plants is at the very heart of the appeal of the garden. People are almost always on the move; gardens are not. Gardens are places where living things are there for us, waiting, accessible, whenever we want them. We do not have to make appointments with gardens. In fact, gardens were here before we were. Eden waited for Adam. Plants existed before animals, whose vast diversity can be explained, in part, by the enormous variety of environmental niches that plants presented. Creatures that could get about on their own steam could eat leaves, drink nectar, bore holes in trunks, consume seeds or make fingerling potato salads with raspberry vinegar and olive oil dressing. Plants are both food and shelter for things that fly, burrow, swim, crawl, slither and walk. For us, they are fuel both for our fires and for our inspiration.

But what is in it for the plants? Is it their lot to be merely the rungs in our evolutionary ladder? Why can't they walk—or run—away from all this rampant consumerism?

If it is a silly question, it has a silly answer: plants do not walk because they do not need to. Why should they bother with that great investment of energy when they can get everything they need in one place? If they could, they might well wonder at all our frantic comings and goings. From where they sit, they net, gather, entice, grab, suck and probe. Thanks to a variety of adaptations, plants can bounce back, as species if not as individuals, from virtually anything that comes their way. They can fend off predators with smelly, bad-tasting oils, with poisons,

irritants, thorns and barks. They can shed leaves in anticipa-
tion of difficult times. As seeds, they can survive fire and flood.
Plants do become extinct, but that is not a sign of inherent weak-
ness; more mobile things become extinct as well.

Another answer to the question exists: photosynthesis does
not provide plants with enough energy for anything beyond a
minimal level of independent movement. Plants are plenty busy
in one spot. There, they are remarkably efficient at turning very
little in the way of visible raw materials into a great deal of matter, a fact proved several centuries ago by van Helmont, a Swiss
chemist. Van Helmont was astonished by the results of his own
experiment. He put 91 kilograms (200 pounds) of dry soil in
a container, moistened it and planted a 2.3-kilogram (5-pound)
willow shoot in it. After five years of giving the willow nothing
but rainwater, he weighed it and found that it was now 74 kilograms (164 pounds). The chemist then dried the soil, weighed
it on its own and found that it was about 57 grams (2 ounces)
lighter than five years earlier. "Thus," he wrote, "the 164
pounds of wood, bark and root arose from the water alone." We
now know that the chemist's conclusions were not quite accu-
rate; 164 pounds of willow came from the energy of sunlight
acting with the water, minerals and air. But the fact remains
that plants live on what humans would consider much less than
a starvation diet. Fifty-seven grams of food would maintain our
body weight for less than a day.

Plants do move—shoots grow, seeds are flung out, roots
reach into the soil, petals close on cloudy days, the leaves of

carnivorous plants close around hapless insects—but they do not change location under their own power. During the stages in which motion away from the parent plant is necessary—shifting pollen from one plant to another or transporting seeds to new territory—plants borrow other things that have independent movement: fluids such as moving air and water and high-octane creatures such as insects, animals and humans. Plants ensure, to an uncanny extent, that these servants are well enough paid and carefully enough directed that they will do exactly what is necessary: take the perfectly ripe pollen from one apple blossom to another apple blossom; deposit the seeds from the raspberry, packed in a little bird-excrement fertilizer, by the hedgerow to germinate.

One might say that in addition to having no feet, plants have no brains, but plants, though undoubtedly brainless, are just as smart as they need to be. Not that they act with deliberation (well, probably not. Scientists shudder at anthropomorphic gardeners, but there is a temptation to think, well, that they think, sort of...), but plants have, obviously, done what they needed to do. They do not need to know how to fly or crawl, make honey or nests, sing or pole-vault, balance a chequebook or make spaceships. Instead, they offer the carbohydrates and proteins, the cellulose, fragrances and colours that allow those things to be done.

Plants are our earthly companions and, more than that, our complements. They are made from the same stuff as we are. They need air, food and water. They use the same minerals as we do. And they are composed of the same proteins, which break down if the temperature becomes too high, causing damage, then death. Their sexual reproduction method is similar to that of animals, with male cells having to make their way to a botanical womb that holds seeds which must be fertilized. The young are given a food supply by the parent to carry them through the initial struggle to establish an independent existence. Plants, like ourselves, have hormones that regulate growth and various stages of maturation. Plants are wounded and heal, they suffer from disease, they struggle, survive and die. . .

We are choosy about what grows in our gardens. Weeds thrive, and we poison them or pull them out, selecting instead more difficult things that must be watered, pruned, dead-headed and then protected in winter. Plant nurseries and seed companies thrive because we gardeners do not want what grows naturally, and furthermore, we fill our gardens not once but over and over.

Most of what we buy dies. Vegetables and flowering annuals meant for a short, productive life in the heat of summer die, but much more of what dies is supposedly longer-lived. Gardeners are forever testing the limits of plant adaptation, intentionally or not, and putting species adapted to warmth into cold places or things adapted to shade into sunny places or things that like rocky ground into wet humus. Even if they are put in the right places, newly planted things left to their own devices, unweeded and unwatered by gardening novices, will probably die.

In the nursery, they thrived and would likely have continued to do so if they could have stayed put. The fact is that plants are just not meant to move about, any more than we are meant to stay rooted. But garden plants must bend to our will and must be lifted, carted, uprooted and transplanted wherever we go. Plants newly arrived in our gardens are very vulnerable. Nothing in millions of years of evolution prepared them for this. So they must be shaded and deeply watered and fussed over until they can make it on their own, more or less.

It would be a great help if a plant could point to the spot where it would like to be or could just get up and walk to that other flower border a few feet away. Then, of course, my entire garden might march next door, where it could be cared for by somebody else. Fortunately for us, plants have no choice but to be endlessly patient with us. They cannot run away when we decide to prune them to look like topknots. They cannot call out when we forget to water them. They cannot hide when we decide to dig them up and cart them to the other side of the path.

And this is why we love them, and love our gardens. Whenever we want to continue our long exploration of what it means to be alive with all the elements that are part of the garden, everything is there, waiting for us. And we are part of the garden too.

THOMAS HARDY IN
HIS GARDEN

BERTIE NORMAN STEPHENS

Bertie Norman Stephens was born in Dorchester, England. After leaving Colliton Street Boys' School he became apprentice gardener on a large estate in Dorset. In 1926, he answered an advertisement for a gardener in the *Dorset Echo* placed by novelist and poet Thomas Hardy (1840–1928). For two years thereafter, Stephens worked at Max Gate, the house Hardy built, caring for the grounds, the chickens, the greenhouse, and the conservatory. This excerpt from Stephens's recollection offers a rare and tantalizing glimpse of Hardy as a shy, restrained man, frail at eighty-six but still writing, a recluse confined to his study and his garden. Hailed at his death as the last of the great Victorians, Hardy, says Stephens, was a kindly, fussy man, most content when he was alone with Nature.

. . .

WHEN I WAS engaged as gardener it was agreed that my duties should consist of the complete control, single-handed, of the one acre of garden and paddock, the greenhouse and conservatory; the cleaning of knives and shoes; the cutting of wood for fires;

the lighting each morning of the boiler to provide hot water for the household, and pumping each morning 500 strokes to fill the house water tanks, and when visitors were in residence, to do additional pumping during the day to ensure an uninterrupted supply of water from the house tanks that were filled from a well. The pump was situated in the kitchen.

My first few weeks at the Max Gate seemed strange to me, as I had been used to working with more than twelve gardeners at Came House, and now was on my own and would have to be responsible for making many gardening decisions and translate into action the wishes of my new employer. On the morning of the day I started at the Hardys' I went round to the kitchen door and tapped. The cook answered my tap and I told her I was the new gardener. She showed me to the garden shed and later Mrs. Hardy came and gave me full instructions for my indoor work, such as shoe cleaning. I knew what to do in the garden without any telling. . .

It was Mr. Hardy's usual habit to leave his study in the middle of the morning and come down to the garden to see me and give me any special instructions relating to planting or collecting crops or blooms. When he was working in his study he wore an eye-shade and a shawl. I could see him from the garden sitting in his study writing, with his eye-shade adjusted. He could look down and see me working in the garden.

Although a naturally placid man he had his moods, and sometimes if he was in one of his bad moods he would not go down to lunch when called. On several occasions I can remember the cook saying to me when I got back from lunch, "The old man's got a bit of a devil on today. He hasn't come down for lunch yet." Sometimes, when Mr. Hardy could not hear we spoke of him as "Old Tom." We often had a change of cook.

He took a great interest in his garden, although he did no active work in it himself. He was too old for that. Between the main entrance to the house and the main gate from the road was a heart-shaped shrubbery in which grew wild plants and flowers such as ferns, primroses and bluebells. Hardy would regularly look at the flowers in this shrubbery and those, also wild, on the banks of the drive. We had many climbing roses in the garden, but no bush or standard roses, as he did not like them. He had a great liking for young asparagus sprouts and all young succulent vegetables. He did not like, and would not have, old vegetables. Sometimes he would himself select and pick a few choice apples or pears for the house. His favourite cooking apple was Lane's Prince Albert, and for his dessert he liked the Charles Ross apple, and the Conference pear.

He was particularly fond of raspberries, and I remember on one occasion he said to me: "I would like a few of those raspberries today, gardener, as I have some friends coming." He also liked strawberries, and had them picked as a special treat for friends who visited him for tea. I had received instructions from Mr. Hardy always to be careful to pick both raspberries and strawberries so that their stems were left on and could be used as little handles to hold the berry and carry it to the mouth when it was being eaten. At no time did Hardy express any appreciation or give any praise for anything that was done in the garden. He took everything for granted. This didn't bother me much. I just took Thomas as my boss and that's all. At the time I worked for him I knew he was famous, but I did not realize he was such a famous man as people believe him to be today. Most Dorchester folk hadn't thought a lot of him. Many had the idea he didn't treat his first wife right...

Although, as I told you earlier, he was usually a very calm man, he could get into a bit of a mood, not actually angry, but irritable, and then when he came down from his study to the garden in one of those moods he would say to me sharply: "I want this or that done, gardener," and then quickly shuffle off across the lawn with his dog Wessex...

The garden was often visited by a hare which somehow managed to get over the wall which surrounded it. It would eat the carrot tops and do a great deal of damage to other growing plants. Wessex used to try and catch it but without any success, and Mr. Hardy, when I told him of its visits and the destruction it caused, said: "I do not mind it in the garden. They are animals, let them carry on." He was very fond of animals and birds, and would never allow me to trap or shoot them however destructive they were to the fruit or vegetables. He insisted that I allow all birds to do as they liked in the garden. This attitude did not always please me, especially when some carefully cultivated fruit was destroyed. We netted the raspberries and strawberries to protect them against birds, but after Mr. Hardy's death Mrs. Hardy employed a builder to erect a permanent fruit cage for the purpose. This was a great improvement and a big saving of time for me.

A path with shrubs on either side of it wound right round the garden and on most mornings after he had studied the weather, which he did every morning when the weather was good enough for him to leave the house, he would walk round this path and examine his favourite flowers and bushes. Again in the evening when the weather was good he made the same journey over the same path. Every Saturday morning it was my job to sweep this path and the one that led from the gate to the house. Hardy liked this done on a Saturday as then the paths were clean and tidy for any visitors who might arrive on the Sunday. He had several favourite spots in the garden, one was near the shrubbery beneath an apple tree down the bottom end. Daffodils, polyanthus, primroses, snowdrops and other flowers grew up through the grass there. He also liked to stand in the conservatory and look out and watch the birds in the pine trees near the green door in the wall which he used when he went out for his walks in the fields. Having tea in the conservatory was another of his enjoyments and there he would sometimes entertain his close friends to tea...

When there were guests at Max Gate Mr. Hardy would give me instructions to be very quiet and I had to creep about the garden like a little worm. No grass cutting could be done, nor any job that made the slightest noise. Mr. Hardy would not allow his visitors to be disturbed. He wanted them to have complete quiet; that quiet which he himself always demanded of life, and that his wife saw that he got...

Hardy was especially fond of spring flowers and some of

his favourites were the primrose, narcissus, daffodil, malmaison carnation, and polyanthus. Some flowers that I grew in the greenhouse were the cyclamen, cineraria, freesia, chrysanthemum (for decorating the dining-room and drawing-room tables), primula, schizanthus, fuchsia, arum lily, and geranium for indoors and summer bedding. On returning from his walks beyond the walls of Max Gate, I often noticed he had a small bunch of wild flowers that he had picked. The only varieties I can remember were primrose, ragged robin, cornflower, and bluebells which he picked in Came Wood.

By late 1927 Mrs. Hardy had to give her husband physical help during his walks in the garden. She would take his arm and together they would slowly walk around the wooded path that encircled the garden. During the last year or so of his life, both Mrs. Hardy and Wessex accompanied him on all his country walks.

At the fall of the year it was desirable to prune or top some of the trees in the garden, but Mr. Hardy always stopped me cutting trees. He would complain that I was cutting far too much and opening up the house to the eyes of the public. He did not like the outside world and wanted to be hidden from it. He was happiest when the trees were thick and tall, casing him in with their greenery. He was not a good mixer and I suppose enjoyed his self-imposed loneliness, shut away so that he could see no one and no one could see him. He liked to be closed in.

On more than one occasion I can remember persons waiting in the house porch all day to get a glimpse of him. If he thought

any member of the public was trying to get a sight of him he
would closely pull the curtains of his study window to avoid
being seen. He went to very great lengths to avoid people, being
a very shy man—unusually shy—shyer than any woman I
have ever met. In my mind's eye I can see him now, with his
ragged old shawl around his neck and shoulders, peeping out of
it, and shuffling round the garden with Wessex his only companion; a never-to-be-forgotten picture of an aged old gentle-
man who was still keenly interested in nature and still studying
for his books...

Within a week or so of Hardy's death there was a grand clear-
ance of his clothes, and masses of letters and other papers from
his study. I was given the task of burning his clothes and bundles
of newspapers on a bonfire in the garden. Mrs. Hardy stood by
the whole time and watched, presumably to ensure that nothing
escaped the flames. All was burnt in her presence except a scarf
which she gave me for my own use. Mrs. Hardy herself burnt, on
another bonfire, baskets full of the letters and private papers that
I had carried down from the study to the garden under her supervision and watchful eye. She would not let me burn these, but
insisted upon doing it herself, and after all the papers had been
destroyed, she raked the ashes to be sure that not a single scrap
or word remained. It was a devil of a clear out. I never knew so
much stuff come out of a room or such a burn up. My impression
was she did not want any of the letters or papers to be seen by
anyone and she was very careful to destroy every trace of them.
I had wondered when she was burning them what had been

among the papers. Had they not been private I should have had them with the clothes and newspapers on my bonfire. Whether she was destroying them on her own initiative or carrying out the wishes of her late husband I never knew, and the world will never learn what went up in flames on that "bonfire day."

ON BEAUTY

HENRI CUECO

Henri Cueco (1929–) was born in the Limousin district of France to a Spanish father and French mother. A teacher and artist, he divides his time between Paris and his country place in Corrèze, where he paints and eats from the small garden made famous in his oddly compelling memoir/novel *Conversations with my Gardener*. Written almost entirely in dialogue, the story ranges from the French countryside to Paris as a painter and his gardener, both men of advancing years, discuss life, death, and the composition of salads. The book is Gallic in its humor and profound discourses: the film based on the book has been described as an al fresco *My Dinner with André*. Unique in form and spirit, this delightful duet pushes the boundaries of garden writing.

. . .

"THERE'S SOMETHING THAT'S been bothering me that I've been wanting to ask you. What's it *for?* I know it's supposed to look beautiful, but where's it meant to go?. . . I've just been wondering. You need space for a big thing like that, so you can step back and look at it. So it has to be the right sort of house. Well heated and that. Not just any old where. Somewhere a bit special."

He is looking with his head bowed.

"It's beautiful . . . if you like that sort of thing. It's all a matter of taste, isn't it? . . . Some people would find it beautiful. I can't tell. Because I've been watching you do it, I'm starting to think it's beautiful. But don't ask me why. Because it's not *for* anything and it's a lot of work, I've been saying to myself, 'It must be beautiful.' But what does that mean? . . . I can't really explain it." *He pondered.* "It gives you pleasure to look at. I can't say more than that, I don't think. The pleasure comes from looking at the colours. It's easier to say what *isn't* beautiful. Now, take that chap who got chopped into pieces by the train yesterday. Did you hear about it? The 13:40 from Paris gets in just before the express that goes *to* Paris. Anyway, the two trains crossed in the station. Only the express didn't stop. This chap gets off the Paris train on the wrong side of the track and gets himself chopped up by the express. No two ways about it, completely mangled him. They found bits of him as far up as the level crossing near the doormat factory. That couldn't have been a pretty sight. Now, you couldn't call that beautiful. It gave him a proper going-over, poor bloke . . . Well, there's no comparison. It's the same words but they're things that have nothing to do with each other. Hmm . . . Poor sod . . . But a painting's not like the real thing. It's how it's made that counts. I can't explain it. You're the professor, not me. I'm happy to watch you. Anyway, I make beautiful things too. Take a look at this."

"What is it?"

"A lettuce."

"That's a lettuce?"

He laughs.

"You see, you're not the only one who makes beautiful things. This is my work."

"It *is* beautiful."

"It's for you. I'm giving it to you. I've got a patch full of them. And I can't eat them all. They'll have bolted by next week."

"Thank you."

"I'll leave it here for you."

"It's a real beauty."

"Beauty means things that give us pleasure to look at. It's simple . . . But what you do is more complicated than a lettuce."

"Perhaps it's not as beautiful."

"I think it's *more* beautiful. Even if I can't say why. With the lettuce, it's because of its crisp white centre, and its size. Whereas with your thing there . . ."

A long pause.

"I'm off for my soup. See you tomorrow. Take care."

"Thanks again for the lettuce."

Translation by George Miller

SEX, SEX, SEX

SHARMAN APT RUSSELL

S harman Apt Russell is a writer from the American Southwest who has explored such diverse territory as American archaeology (*When the Land was Young,* 1996), the mythology of the New West (*Kill the Cowboy,* 1993), and the natural history of the region (*Songs of the Fluteplayer,* 1991). Her first novel, *The Last Matriarch* (2000), was set in paleolithic New Mexico. With the publication of *Anatomy of a Rose: Exploring the Secret Life of Flowers* (2001), she broadened her focus. Ranging from memoir to a survey of scientific thinking on every aspect of floriculture, these essays, excerpted below, are both intimate and intellectually intriguing. She makes a strong case for learning the idiosyncrasies and habits of what we grow: "Unknowing, we are not much more than blind voyeurs."

. . .

THE JACK-IN-THE-PULPIT IS considering a sex change. The violets have a secret. The dandelion is smug. The daffodils are obsessive. The orchid is *finally* satisfied, having produced over a million seeds. The bellflower is *not* satisfied and is slowly bending its stigma in order to reach its own pollen. The pansies wait expectantly, their vulviform faces lifted to the sky. The evening primrose is interested in one thing and one thing only.

A stroll through the garden is almost embarrassing.

ABOUT 80 percent of flowers are hermaphrodites, both male and female. Pollination is the movement of pollen from an anther to a stigma. Fertilization occurs when the sperm from a pollen grain unites with an egg in the ovary.

Hermaphrodite flowers could easily pollinate and fertilize themselves. Most don't. Instead, they try to mix and match their pollen and eggs with the pollen and eggs from flowers of the same species: I'll take this. You take that. Here. Yes.

Sex, good sex, is all about cross-fertilization. Why?

Why have sex at all?

In terms of the individual and its offspring, asexual reproduction is so much easier. You don't have to think about males or male parts. You cut your investment in half. You don't have to use up all that energy and time. You just reproduce.

In a sexual population, an asexual mutant has many advantages and should quickly spread and take over. In an asexual population, a sexual mutant has many disadvantages and should quickly die out.

Scientists are still puzzled by the question: What good is sex?

They have some theories.

In a cell, when genes divide and replicate themselves, their occasional changes or mistakes are sometimes harmful and even lethal. But when an individual gets a set of genes from two different parents, that dangerous mutation can be neutralized. The normal form of the gene usually takes over, and the mutation is not expressed. In the offspring of asexual reproduction, the harmful genes tend to accumulate.

The recombination of genes from two different parents also allows for diversity among offspring. For natural selection to work, the genetic recombination has to create an immediate advantage for those individuals. In a variable world, their variability may mean that more of them survive.

Finally, there is the theory of the long run. Natural selection would not favour sex or cross-fertilization because these things are good for the species. Natural selection does not care about the future of the species. But sex and cross-fertilization *are* good for the species because they prevent the buildup of harmful mutations and because they produce a population that is diverse. When the climate gets colder, when pollinators disappear, when new diseases attack, the population may have individuals that can survive and reproduce. In the long run, species lucky enough to be sexual—species that, for complex reasons, resist asexuality—may simply be the ones that last.

THESE ARE only theories. But you're convinced. You decide to be sexual. And you decide to cross-fertilize.

First, you must avoid clogging up your stigma with your own pollen grains.

Some flowers, like delphinium, separate their sexual parts in time. In a version of cross-dressing, they go through a male stage, when their anthers produce pollen. Then, in a matter of hours or days, they go through a female stage, when the stigma is ready to receive pollen. In the passionflower, the stigmas curve down at this point, bending back to fit between their own anthers, closer now to the colored mosaic of petals, closer now to the pollinating bee.

A few flowers reverse the process, stigma first, anthers second.

Flowers also separate their parts in space. In many flowers, the stigma rises well above the encircling stamens. An insect first plops on the stigma as a good place to land, deposits its pollen, and then goes exploring, rummaging around the petals, and collecting new pollen. In the rockrose, the anthers are sensitive to touch. Once a pollinator has visited the flower, the anthers splay down and away from the central stigma.

The position of these organs is never casual.

Some plants have two sexes, much like animals. The willow has a male form with flowers that only have stamens and a female form with flowers that only have stigmas. There is a Mr. and Mrs. Mistletoe, a Mr. and Mrs. Stinging Nettle, a Mr. and Mrs. Cottonwood, and a Mr. and Mrs. Holly. This is the most dramatic separation of parts.

Some plants have two sexes but on the same inflorescence. Other species mix up their inflorescences with hermaphrodite flowers, male flowers, and female flowers.

Plants juggle their sexual parts and move around their sexes as a way of avoiding self-pollination.

A few plants also have the ability to choose their sex. An individual bog myrtle will produce only female flowers one year and only male flowers the next. It's not indecision. The myrtle is responding to water or nutrients in the soil, to light, or to temperature. Commonly, female flowers require more resources and more time to produce fruit; in a difficult situation, a plant reasonably decides to be male.

A young jack-in-the-pulpit is often male in its first season. When it is bigger and stronger, when it has stored up a supply of starch, it will consider the more ambitious female lifestyle.

A SINGLE FLOWER GENUS can show the range of sexual strategy. The large, showy lady's smock (*Cardamine pratensis*) is cross-pollinated by many insects and is largely self-incompatible. The small bittercress (*C. amara*) is pollinated by flies and is easily capable of self-fertilization. The smaller hairy bittercress (*C. hirsuta*) is a habitual selfer.

Flowers are flexible. Flowers are determined.

The flower of a European orchid resembles the female of a certain bee. In parts of the Mediterranean, the flowers of a related species are grabbed by a lusty male bee and pollinated. But when the bee died out in western Europe, the orchid evolved into a habitual selfer. Now, a few days after the flower has opened, its polinia (masses or sacs of pollen attached to a stem) lazily fall out of the anther, hang in front of the stigma, and wait for a breeze.

Give that orchid a pollinator and it would return to cross-breeding. If that pollinator looked like a helicopter instead of a bee, the flower would consider the situation.

We humans do as strange—or stranger—things for sex.

PEONIES

ELEANOR PERÉNYI

Eleanor Perényi had only two gardens in her life: the *jardin anglais* that surrounded the castle of the Hungarian baron she married at nineteen in 1937 (and wrote about in the memoir *More was Lost,* 1946) and the Connecticut garden she took up with reluctance and to which she became quite attached. She worked all her life in magazines, as an editor at *Mademoiselle* and *Harper's Bazaar,* and as a contributor to *The Atlantic Monthly, Harper's,* and *Esquire,* but it was her garden in Stonington, Connecticut, that was her avocation and her greatest pleasure. Developed over thirty years, it was the inspiration for *Green Thoughts: A Writer in the Garden* (1981), which has become a staple of garden literature, written in a forthright, irreverent tone that is perennially fresh.

· · ·

A FASHION PHOTOGRAPHER I once knew, famous in her day, was in due course obliged to retire to a farm, thereby causing much anxiety to her friends. What, they wondered, would this dynamic woman, whose perfectionism had terrorized the studio, do with her old age? She took to raising tree peonies, and these beautiful, temperamental plants clearly came to replace the models she had alternately bullied and coaxed to do their best for so many years. I last saw her in her potting shed, surrounded by notebooks in which she recorded the genealogies of her favorites, absorbed in questions of drainage and soil, happy as only the obsessed can be; I have no doubt that her peonies, not in bloom at the time, were faultless. They are, as everyone familiar with their images in Oriental paintings, silks and porcelains knows, among the world's loveliest flowers, at once sumptuous and subtle in their golds and moonlight-pinks and snowy whites; their finely cut foliage makes that of the common, herbaceous peonies look coarse. They are in short the royalties of the peony world; and perhaps for that very reason I have come to feel they belong to these gardeners with a streak of fanatacism, to whom the shortcomings of the race are a challenge rather than an annoyance, the kind of person who will cherish a plant for twenty years for the sake of a few, jewel-like flowers—someone like my friend.

I am not of that order. I have a few tree peonies but am in no sense a connoisseur, and I have several objections to them. To begin with, and on all but one of my plants, these dazzling flowers are nearly invisible, hidden beneath the foliage. To admire them I must cut them and they don't make good cut flowers. The heads are too heavy for the short, flimsy stems, and so they end up in shallow bowls or in a bud vase, not my preferred ways of arranging flowers. (The exception is "Renkaku," meaning "fight of cranes," a Japanese variety, white and the size of a dinner plate—which, however, and contrary to its reputation, flowers so sparsely that in a decade it has never reproduced more than three blossoms in a season, and its upright, solid stalks can't quite make up for such a parsimonious habit.) Nor do any of them have much scent—that of the white, faint as it is, is distinctly rank, rather like a mushroom going bad.

It has, of course, occurred to me that something is wrong with the way I grow them—though I can't think what. The plants are large and healthy, if scarcely to be described as trees. That is a misnomer. Tree peonies are small shrubs with a woody skeleton that doesn't die down in winter as the stalks of the herbaceous peonies do. I have been told that the two shouldn't be grown in the same bed, though no such warning is given in books and their requirements (rich soil, good drainage, shelter from wind, etc.) are as far as I know identical. Mine, however, *are* planted together, and if that is a mistake, the purveyors ought to say so.

But I am beginning to think that the small group of people involved in the breeding, propagating and selling of tree peonies in this country must constitute a tight little island of specialists catering to other specialists, without much interest in communicating with the rest of us... The inbred nature of the tree-peony business, which together with the understandably sky-high prices of the plants (tree peonies are propagated by grafting and a minimum of five years is needed to judge success or failure) makes for a kind of exclusivity that doesn't feel the need to explain itself. The onus is on the outsider who tries to get into the club, usually by the back door.

A back door exists. Tree peony plants are often sold at garden centers—packed in cardboard cartons and unlabeled as to variety; also by mass-production nurseries who classify them by color only. These cost a fraction of the cultivars offered by nurseries specializing in tree peonies—and by rights should be correspondingly inferior. With plants as with everything else you usually get what you pay for. Not with tree peonies. Not only do the prices vary wildly within the precincts of the club . . . but there is no assurance that a plant, picked up at a garden center or ordered from a third-class source, will be a whit less beautiful or prolific than a pedigreed cultivar. All it may lack is a guaranteed lineage, a name.

I don't approve of the situation. I only say it exists, and in proof I offer the distressing fact that the most beautiful tree peony I own came from just such a dubious source some years ago, at a cost of $7.95. At the time, I didn't know what it was, and didn't care. I now realize that it is a *lutea* hybrid and a rare one at that, on account of its green-gold color. The *luteas* are the only truly yellow peonies, but none I have seen is this extraordinary shade or has this form: globular and heavy in the hand as a ball of silk. It lasts longer, too, than one of its pedigreed relatives I own, Souvenir de Maxime Cornu, a rumpled yellow edged with crimson—which is to say that it may survive as long as five days in water before it shatters, as all peonies do, overnight, casting its petals all over the ebony surface of the piano and revealing, like a peach, a bloodstained heart. And while I am on the subject, I should also mention an anonymous white, apparently a duplicate of the "flight of cranes," purchased I don't remember where, which covers itself with bloom and for which I can't have paid more than $10.

I am not doubting the integrity of those who dedicate their lives and fortunes to the breeding and propagation of tree peonies. I am suggesting that something is wrong with the way the business is regulated, and the plants themselves defined. When I pay a steep price for a named cultivar I ought to be getting more than a fancy title: the plant itself should perform better than the anonymous specimen costing less than half as much; and mine just don't. In the last analysis I'm not even prepared to say they are more beautiful than the common herbaceous peonies that everybody grows and nobody makes a fuss about. They are less varied in form and color, and if a display of great big gorgeous flowers is what you are after, the herbaceous peonies are my choice.

The herbaceous peonies stand straight and tall, don't hide their heads and are magnificent for cutting. They aren't temperamental, deciding, for inscrutable reasons, to withhold their bloom for a year. They are almost immortal, even when hopelessly neglected in the backyards of old farms. They can stand temperatures below zero. Tree peonies are sturdy too, but because they don't die to the ground as herbaceous peonies do, their superstructure is liable to winter damage. Often, in fact,

they will look quite dead at the end of a bad winter, tempting
you to cut back the wood. Don't. Concealed in a scaly brown
casing is a pink bud that if no permanent damage has been done
will burst forth when the proper time comes. All peonies suffer
when a heavy rain hits them, and by the law of averages a deluge
will occur at least once in the blooming season. Heavy rain will
ruin the more delicate blossoms of the tree peonies, which don't
like hot, bright sun either—and I hear of gardeners who place
open umbrellas over their plants to protect them, a quaint effect
perhaps, if the umbrellas were Japanese parasols, but can you
imagine doing it? To such lengths I will not go, and with herbaceous peonies need not. They love sun, and after a rain need
only be given a good shake to revive.

Colette says, "The peony smells of peonies, that is to say of
cockchafers," and only she would know what cockchafers smell
like. Lilacs, she further says, have the "discreet smell of scarab
beetles," whatever that may be. I am not good at such com-
parisons. Peony scents vary greatly, from one so like a rose I
couldn't in the dark, tell the difference, to an acrid sweetness not
unlike the lilac's. The doubles smell better than the singles and
the herbaceous better than the tree peonies—to me. As with
roses, one is confronted with stark divergences of opinion. The
authors of *The Fragrant Year* say all the Japanese tree peonies
have scent, the more perfumed of them "a yeasty sweetness that
shades from narcotic and repelling to something quite delightful." Never having visited a great tree-peony collection (for
example, that at Swarthmore College in Pennsylvania, which is

said to have over two hundred named varieties), I can only retort that mine don't—and that includes Souvenir de Maxime Cornu, which they think outstandingly sweet. They also find the odor of the old-fashioned Memorial Day peony, *Paeonia officinalis*, "unbearable," and I don't agree about that either. (Is this perhaps Colette's cockchafer-scented flower?) Further, I notice that today's catalogues haven't a word to say about scent, from which I conclude, perhaps wrongly, that the modern hybrids have little or no perfume. But as I never buy them, I can't say.

That may or may not be one of the drawbacks to peonies. Once you have them, you have them for a lifetime and you can pass them along to your grandchildren, which makes for an unadverturous spirit. Unless you have occasion to start a fresh collection, there is no incentive other than curiosity to buy new plants. Most of my herbaceous peonies have been in place for the better part of forty years, quite long enough for me to have forgotten what they are—or what is more reprehensible, to try to find out. Trying to identify them would be rather like suddenly asking your oldest friend his mother's maiden name. To me, they are just peonies: double pinks, whites dribbled with crimson, shell-colored singles with golden hearts, ruby-reds. Having had them so long, I can predict almost to the hour when they will come into bloom—beginning with the tremendous pink ball at the fence corner—and nearly as accurately when they will come to an end, six weeks later. (The tree peonies, blooming earlier, are less predictable. Sometimes they overlap their herbaceous cousins, sometimes not.)

Yet his predictability is not a bore. One looks forward to the peony season as to the yearly visit of friends one loves, and the impulse to go whoring after novelties is, in me, quickly stilled. I could no more dig up these old friends and replace them with new ones than I could tell a human being that after thirty or forty years I was tired of his company. Moreover, peonies (of either type) need time to settle down and do justice to their capacities. Properly cared for, which is a simple matter of enough water and plenty of fertilizer/mulch, they improve with age like wine, and if you have a clump you like, my advice is to leave it be. Given the unavoidable hazards of gardening, the droughts and killing winters, the attacks of insects, a perennial that is immune to all of them is a godsend.

POPPYCOCK

DES KENNEDY

D es Kennedy (1945–) is a philosopher and former monk who claims
he "left his order for an even greater calling." A witty, iconoclas-
tic gardener, Kennedy has worked his eleven acres on Denman Island off
British Columbia's coast for thirty-six years, culling that plot of land for
three books of essays, including *An Ecology of Enchantment: A Year in a
Country Garden* (1998), excerpted here. A committed environmentalist, he
is also a novelist (*The Garden Club*, 1996) and an award-winning journalist
and broadcaster, co-writer of the documentary series *Reinventing the World*.
Erudite and slightly off-centre, he says he is living proof of e. e. cummings's
line that "not for philosophers does this rose give a damn."

. . .

OUR GARDENS ARE ablaze with poppies at present, and
there's no more perilous interlude in the gardening year. Unde-
niably exquisite, unquestionably evocative of ineffable sentiments, poppies are also notorious for provoking more outlandish

behaviour and florid oratory than a senator gone to the bottle. The Papavers put people over the top in a way that few other flowers—indeed, few other life forms—can. We may linger overlong over our daylilies, we may on occasion be a tad too effusive about our fuchsias, but neither produces the fantastic excesses that poppies do.

Just listen to the language that gets flounced about as soon as a poppy or two pops open. "The acme of grace," Louise Beebe Wilder calls them, while you're chatting together at an intimate gathering, "the best of laughter, the rarest embodiment of all that is delightsome, careless, touchingly fugitive." All true enough in its own way, of course, you couldn't agree more. Just as you're going to add a clever observation about the frothy charms of filipendula, Celia Thaxter bustles over and begins waxing about how poppies produce "splendour so dazzing as to baffle all powers of description." Quite so, but this doesn't deter some people from trying to describe them anyway. Among the worst is old John Ruskin, who can sniff out a poppy conversation the way turkey vultures can scent carrion. Here he comes now, sauntering across the room, as though by chance. Seldom stuck for words, Ruskin shakes his wattles, strikes a meaningful pose and solemnly intones: "The poppy is painted glass; it never glows so brightly as when the sun shines through it. Whenever it is seen against the light or with the light, it is a flame, and warms the mind like a blown ruby."

The old blowhard really is overstating it a bit, having a mind warmed "like a blown ruby," but these ostentations are commonplace in poppy talk. By this point you begin getting an uncomfortable feeling, as when you're cornered at a party by someone who specializes in psychobabble. You take to scanning the room for escape routes. But Ruskin, once he's got the wind in his sails, is not one to shut up. "It is an intensely simple, intensely floral flower," he tells you knowingly. You presume that an "intensely floral flower" is much like an intensely choral choir, but refrain from saying so, in the hope that the conversation will peter out. No such luck. "All silk and flame," he carries on, staring raptly at a point well above your head, so that you wonder if he's talking to you, or to God, or simply to posterity. "A scarlet cup, perfect edged all round, seen among the wild grass far away like a burning coal fallen from heaven's altars."

Blown rubies and now burning coals to boot, this has gone just about far enough. You begin subtly scuttling sideways, like a crab, towards the nearest exit. But the old codger, more nimble than you'd expect, cuts you off with a small but effective countermove and carries on. "You cannot have a more complete, a more stainless type of flower absolute," he tells you. Or a more tedious conversation, you're thinking to yourself, now pinned against the draperies. "Inside and outside, all flower. No sparing of colour anywhere, no outside coarseness, no interior secrecies, open as the sunshine that creates it..." Swept up in his old prose, the old duffer closes his eyes to ponder the magical effect he's conjured, giving you just enough time to slip sideways and away.

But there's no sure sanctuary from bizarre encounters at poppy time. Ducking through the kitchen, you bump once again into the always-charming Celia Thaxter. "The orange of the Iceland poppy," she exclaims out of nowhere, "is the most ineffable colour." You would have thought that ineffable was not subject to gradation: that to be "most ineffable" is rather like being most pregnant, but never mind. "It is orange dashed with carmine," Celia blushes, "most like the reddest coals of an intensely burning fire." Poppy talk is full of fires and flames. You agree with her wholeheartedly, discreetly lift a glass of punch from her silver tray and keep moving.

Over in another corner, Robert Browning's holding court. You overhear him proclaim "the poppy's red effontery," at which his clutch of gathered admirers all sigh. You do a quick 180 degree turn, only to run right into Louise Beebe Wilder again. Such a character, Louise. The talk quickly turns from Shirley poppies to California poppies which she describes as "fore-gathered in blithe haphazardry." Rather than routing every-one within earshot, this peculiar figure of speech attracts Celia Thaxter back over. As dear as she is to all of us, poor Celia can't help herself when it comes to California poppies. She launches immediately into a soliloquy, having first handed you the serv-ing tray so as to leave her hands free for illustrative gesturing. "It is held upright on a straight and polished stem," she tells us, not for the first time, "its petals curving upward and outward into the cup of light, pure gold with a lustrous satin sheen; a rich orange is painted on the gold"—here she makes delicate painterly gestures—"drawn in infinitely fine lines to a point in the centre of the edge of each petal, so that the effect is that of a diamond of flame in a cup of gold." We've already had Ruskin's warmed rubies, we may as well have Celia's flaming diamonds as well. "It is not enough that the powdery anthers are orange bordered with gold; they are whirled about the very heart of the flower like a revolving Catherine-wheel of fire"—she whirls her right hand histrionically, almost spilling the drinks. "In the centre of the anthers is a shining point of warm sea-green, a last, consummate touch which makes the beauty of the blossom supreme." She finishes speaking, her uplifted face flushed with rapture. Even Louise is uncharacteristically at a loss for words. You have the disconcerting sense of being out of your depth, floundering in a sea of flaming jewels.

In the cold and sober light of dawn you might be inclined to dismiss all this purple poppy prose as of no consequence. Surely, you say to yourself, horse people or Harley-Davidson people are every bit as fanatical in their enthusiasms, and who's the worse for it? But not so. Like the tormented souls who end up stalking movie stars, poppy admirers soon stumble from devotion into delusion. Opium and field poppies are often their undoing, for these thrive as brilliant itinerants, nomads that wander wherever they will, self-seeding abundantly, hybridizing recklessly and popping up in stunning new colours all over the map. They are a wild bunch, far beyond anyone's control, free spirits that will not tolerate the fusty rituals of horticulture. The less you do for these vagabonds the better.

Fair enough. The only trouble being that admiring gardeners can begin believing that they themselves are kindred free
spirits. They tumble headlong into the delusion that they too
are colourful gypsies at heart, unfettered by mortgages, careers
or compost heaps, free to wander the wild hills and fields, perhaps lingering for a while beneath the shady oak to play the
pan pipes and take what beauty they may. There's no need to
belabour the point: this is daydreaming of an entirely frivolous
and potentially catastrophic sort. Who's looking after the summer pruning while all this merry pipe-playing's going on? Who
exactly is picking, shelling and freezing the peas while everyone's off cavorting as free spirits? With a list of chores longer
than the road to Mandalay, the gardener risks everything by
idle fantasizing about life as a carefree gypsy rover.

A bad end awaits. Flaming silken petals fall in due course
from the opium poppies, revealing statuesque seed heads, each
balanced like a tiny urn on a tall stalk. Now a seductive danger
slithers in as the gardener, long since accepting that the open
road of whimsy inevitably curves back around to the potting
shed, begins musing on Dryden's "sleepy poppies." Their flowers have carried us to heights of ecstasy scarcely otherwise
imaginable. Intoxicated, we now decide, with poor pathetic
Coleridge and all the rest, to enter the ancient pleasure dome
through a tiny slit in their seed heads. Even Celia Thaxter, of
all people, the very embodiment of gardening respectability,
found herself under their spell: "I muse over their seed pods,"
she confided in me as the party was winding down, "those

supremely graceful urns that are wrought with such match-
less elegance of shape, and think what strange power they hold
within. Sleep is there, and Death his brother, imprisoned in
those mystic sealed cups."

Best to leave them sealed, Celia darling. Set those precarious
yearnings aside. We have glimpsed the splendours of Xanadu in
the brief and glowing brilliance of the flower. It is enough. Now
go to sleep and dream.

A FEW HINTS
ON GARDENING

CATHARINE PARR TRAILL

Catharine Parr Traill (1802–1899) started writing children's books
at sixteen, producing one a year until 1832 when she left England
with her husband to homestead in Upper Canada near her sister, Susanna
Moodie. Traill described her pioneer life in letters and diaries, which she
collected and published as *The Backwoods of Canada* (1836). This was followed by several novels and botanical works, particularly *Canadian Wild
Flowers* (1868) and *Studies of Plant life in Canada* (1885). Concerned about
the ability of women to survive in the bush—and to grow sufficient food
for their families—she gathered her best advice into *The Female Emigrant's
Guide* (1854), later retitled *The Canadian Settler's Guide* (1855), excerpted
here in a piece that illuminates Traill's remarkable resourcefulness and her
lifelong love of plants.

. . .

APRIL IN CANADA is not the same month in its general fea-
tures, as the lovely, showery, capricious April, that month of
smiles and tears, of storms and sunshine, in dear old England.

137

It is often cold, stern and harsh, yet with many hopeful changes that come to cheat us into the belief that winter is gone, and the season of buds and flowers is at hand, and some years it is so; but only once in five or ten years does the Canadian April prove a pleasant genial month.

Some warm, lovely, even sultry days, misty like Indian summer, are experienced, and the snow melts rapidly and a few flies creep out and sport awhile in the warm beams of the young sun, but "by-and-by a cloud takes all away." The wind blows chilly, snow showers fall, and all is cold, cheerless winter again.

In fine Aprils a few blossoms peep out from under the thick carpet of dead leaves, and then you see the pretty snow-flower or Hepatica lifting its starry head and waving in the spring breezes on the waysides, on upturned roots and in the shelter of the underwood where the forest is a little thinned out so as to admit the warm beams of the sun; pale pink, blue of two shades, and snowy white are the varieties of this cheerful little flower. Violets, the small white, and a few pale blue ones, are next seen. The rich rank soil at the edges of your clearing produces the sanguinaria or blood-root—the modest white flower shrouded at its first breaking the soil in a vine-shaped leaf, veined with orange. The root of this plant affords a bright red dye to the Indians, with which they stain the bark of their mats and baskets. You may know the blood-root, on breaking the leaf or the root, by its red juice.

In low, open, moist ground the mottled leaf of the dog's-tooth violet *(Erythronium)* comes up, and late in April the yellow bells, striped on the outside of the petal with purplish brown, come up in abundance. Spring-beauty, too, is an April flower, a delicate little flower with pale pink striped bell— *Claytonia* is its botanical name—but we love to call these wild flowers by some simple name, which simple folks may easily remember.

As the snow melts off in the woods, the leaves of various evergreen plants appear still fresh and green. Among these are the Pyrolas or sweet-wintergreens, a numerous and lovely family of Canadian plants; several varieties of the club-moss, one of which is known as the festoon pine, and is used to make wreaths for ornamenting the settlers' houses with. The wild garlic, too, shows its bright green spear-shaped leaves early in this month. This plant so eagerly sought for by the cattle to which it is a very healing medicine, is dreaded by the dairy-maid, as it destroys the flavour of the milk and spoils the butter.

If the month of April should prove cold, many of the above named flowers put off their blossoming time, appearing in the ensuing month of May.

April unlocks the ice-bound lakes, and streams; and it is during this month, that the winter snows are dissolved: the warmth which in sunnier climes brings to perfection the bulbs, and gives odour to the violet and blue bell, the pale primrose, and the narcissus, here must be expended in loosing the frost-bound earth from its icy fetters, and the waters from their frozen chains. Let us therefore not despise our Canadian April, though she be not as winning and fair as her namesake at home . . .

A FEW HINTS ON GARDENING

Owing to the frosts and chilling winds that prevail during the month of April, and often into the early part of May, very little work is done in the garden excepting it be in the matter of planting out trees and bushes; grafting and pruning, and preparing the ground by rough digging or bringing in manure. The second week in May is generally the time for putting in all kinds of garden seeds: any time from the first week in May to the last, sowing may be carried on. Kidney beans are seldom quite secure from frost before the 25th. I have seen both beans, melons, and cucumbers cut off in one night, when they were in six or eight leaves. If the season be warm and showery early sowing may succeed, but unless guarded by glass, or oiled-paper frames, the tender vegetables should hardly be put in the open ground before the 18th or 20th May: corn is never safe before that time. The coldness of the ground and the sharpness of the air, in some seasons, check vegetation, so that the late sowers often succeed better than they who put the seeds in early. Having given some directions in various places about planting corn, potatoes, melons, and some other vegetables, I shall now add a few memoranda that may be useful to the emigrant-gardener. If you wish to have strong and early cabbage-plants, sow in any old boxes or even old sugar-troughs, putting some manure at the bottom, and six or eight inches of good black leaf-mould on the top, and set in a sunny aspect. The plants thus sown will not be touched by the fly. If sown later in May, set your trough on some raised place, and water them from time to time. Or you may sow on the open ground, and sprinkle wood-ashes or soot over the ground: this will protect the plants. The fly also eats off seedling tomatoes, and the same sprinkling will be necessary to perserve them.

In sowing peas, single rows are better in this country than double ones, as unless there be a good current of air among the plants they are apt to be mildewed.

Lettuces sow themselves in the fall, and you may plant them out early in a bed, where they will have the start of those sown in the middle of May.

Those who have a root-house or cellar usually store their cabbages in the following way: they tie several together by the stem near the root, and then hang them across a line or pole head downwards: others pit them head downwards in a pit in the earth, and cover them first with dry straw and then with earth above that. The stem with the root should be stored by till spring, when if planted out, they will afford good, early, tender greens at a season when vegetables are not to be had.

There are many substitutes for greens used in Canada. The most common one is the Wild Spinach, better known by its local name of Lamb's-quarter. It grows spontaneously in all garden grounds, and may be safely used as a vegetable. It is tender, and when thrown into boiling water with a little salt, and cooked for five minutes, and drained, and set to the table like spinach, is much esteemed by the country people.

The Mayweed, a large yellow ranunculus that grows in marshy wet places, is also freely used: but be careful to use no wild plant unless you have full assurance of its being wholesome and that no mistake has been made about it. There is another wild green called Cow-cabbage that is eaten, but this also requires an experienced settler to point it out.

It is always well to save your own seeds if you can. A few large carrots should be laid by to plant out early in Spring for seed. Onions the same, also beets, parsnips, and some of your best cabbages. Seeds will always fetch money at the stores, if good and fresh, and you can change with neighbours.

If you have more than a sufficiency for yourself do not begrudge a friend a share of your superfluous garden seeds. In a new country like Canada a kind and liberal spirit should be encouraged; in out-of-the-way, country places people are dependent upon each other for many acts of friendship. Freely ye will receive, freely give, and do not forget the advice given in the scriptures, "Use hospitality one to another," and help one another when you see any one in distress; for these are opportunities cast in your way by God himself, and He will require the use or abuse of them at your hands.

SKYRRETS OF PERU

JOHN GERARD

John Gerard (1545–1612) was a barber-surgeon who tended a "physick" garden on Fetterlane in London. An avid collector of rare plants, he published a list of the species he grew in 1596, the first complete catalogue of the contents of a garden. A year later, the famous herbal that bears his name was released. Experts now believe it to be an English translation of a Dutch herbal by Rembert Dodoen, with species added from Gerard's garden and from North American explorations, including the first published description of the potato, excerpted here. Despite its clouded origins, Gerard's *Herball* stands as a landmark of botanical publishing, and when Thomas Johnson, a London apothecary, corrected and expanded the book in 1633, it became the gold standard of horticultural texts for two hundred years.

. . .

THIS PLANT (which is called of some Skyrrets of Peru) is generally of us called Potatus or Potato's. It hath long rough flexible branches trailing upon the ground like unto those of

Pompions, whereupon are set greene three cornered leaves very like those of the wilde Cucumber.

The roots are many, thicke, and knobby, like unto the roots of Peonies, or rather of the white Asphodill, joined together at the top into one head, in manner of the Skyrret, which being divided into divers parts and planted, do make a great increase, especially if the greatest roots be cut into divers goblets, and planted in good and fertile ground.

The Potato's grow in India, Barbarie, Spaine, and other hot regions; of which I planted divers roots (which I bought at the Exchange in London) in my garden, where they flourished until winter, at which time they perished and rotted.

The Potato roots are among the Spaniards, Italians, Indians, and many other nations, ordinarie and common meat; which no doubt are of mighty and nourishing parts, and doe strengthen and comfort nature; whose nutriment is as it were a mean between flesh and fruit, but somewhat windie; yet being roasted in the embers they lose much of their windinesse, especially being eaten sopped in wine.

Of these roots may be made conserves no lesse toothsome, wholesome, and dainty, than of the flesh of Quinces; and likewise those comfortable and delicate meats called in shops, *Morselli, Placentulae,* and divers other such like.

These roots may serve as a ground or foundation whereon the cunning Confectioner or Sugar-Baker may worke and frame many comfortable delicat Conserves and restorative sweet-meats.

They are used to be eaten rosted in the ashes. Some when they be so rosted infuse and sop them in wine: and others to give them the greater grace in eating, do boile them with prunes and so eat them: likewise others dress them (being first rosted) with oile, vineger, and salt, every man according to his owne taste and liking. Notwithstanding howsoever they be dressed, they comfort, nourish, and strengthen the body.

POTATO'S OF VIRGINIA

Virginian Potato hath many hollow flexible branches trailing upon the ground, three square, uneven, knotted or kneed in sundry places at certain distances: from the which knots cometh forth one great leafe made of divers leaves, some smaller, and others greater, set together upon a fat middle rib by couples, of a swart greene colour tending to rednesse; the whole leafe resembling those of the Winter-Cresses, but much larger; in taste at the first like grasse, but afterward sharp and nipping the tongue. From the bosome of which leaves come forth long round slender footstalkes, whereon grow very fair and pleasant floures.

It groweth naturally in America, where it was first discovered, as reporteth *Clusius,* since which time I have received roots hereof from Virginia, otherwise called Norembega, which grow & prosper in my garden as in their owne native country.

The Indians call this plant *Pappus,* meaning the roots; by which name also the common Potatoes are called in those Indian countries. Wee have it's proper name mentioned in the title.

The vertues be referred to the common Potato's, being likewise a food, as also a meat for pleasure, equall in goodnesse and wholesomnesse to the same, being either rosted in the embers, or boiled and eaten with oile, vineger and pepper, or dressed some other way by the hand of a skilfull Cooke.

LETTERS TO A
GARDENING FRIEND

KATHARINE S. WHITE AND
ELIZABETH LAWRENCE

C redited by William Shawn as the person who "gave *The New Yorker* its shape and set it on its course," Katharine S. White (1892–1977) started work at the magazine six months after its founding in 1925 and became its first fiction editor, staying thirty-six years to nurture writers such as Vladimir Nabokov, John Updike, and E. B. White, whom she married. In 1958, she wrote the first of her *New Yorker* columns (posthumously collected and published as *Onward and Upward in the Garden*). Elizabeth Lawrence (1904–1985) sent a fan letter in response to the column, thus initiating a correspondence that continued until White's death. A newspaper garden columnist and author of four books, including the classic *A Southern Garden* (1942), Lawrence is now recognized as one of America's best garden writers. These two intelligent, private women, devoted to their gardens in Maine and North Carolina, are exquisitely revealed in *Two Gardeners: A Friendship in Letters,* excerpted here. "I wish you lived next door," Elizabeth wrote to Katharine, "I would fill your garden up."

[June 1962]

Dear Katharine,

I was so happy to find your letter in the mail. I have kept up with you through Mr. Ranger, who wrote that you were home, and better, and doing another "Onward and Upward." *The New Yorker* came the next day, and the piece is wonderful. I took it to Hannah Withers who was equally pleased, and is even more indignant than you over Mrs. H's [Buckner Hollingsworth's] portrait of Miss Jekyll. I feel sure that most authors would consider that you had given *Her Garden Was Her Delight* a very good review... We both think Mrs. H. would have done a better job to leave Miss Jekyll and Mrs. Loudon out, and to have put in two other American women—Mrs. Wilder, for example. Hannah was so pleased over your devotion to Hedrick... She said, "That's what I like about Mrs. White, she likes all the books I like..."

My mother continues to go downhill very slowly. She gets more weary and I get more depressed. I am not taking on any new clients for a while, but I have to help old ones, and friends, and that and the garden and my column and the nursing leave me little time or strength to concentrate on writing. I don't see how you do what you do... or rather I do see. You are better disciplined.

Mary's husband, who is as good as she is, has been helping me in the garden when his boss-man doesn't require him on his afternoon off, but I can't turn him loose, and even standing beside him could not prevent his pulling up a hellebore—a rare one—that was just getting established...

I was so interested in what you said about bamboos. Would you like me to send you a root of mine? It is the one that Elsie Hassan grows in Ohio, though the government people said they could not name it for me. Elsie says hers has come through that zero weather last winter—though, of course, it suffered...

My book is a sort of medley—more of the same—about my friends in person and in books—especially "Elizabeth" [von Arnim] of whom I have written so much in my column as well as in my books. No one else has ever written of gardens as she has—it must have been hard to be her child or her husband or servant, but they all seem to have adored her. It was only her lovers who got the upper hand...

I am a non-sprayer. Too lazy, and using poison scares me stiff. We find dead and dying birds every summer when the DDT wagon makes its round. But we also have fewer flies and bugs.

Let me know if you still want your hellebores. And if you know how hardy the chinquapin rose is. But don't bother to tell me, if the answer is no.

Aff,

Elizabeth Lawrence

June 25, 1962

Dear Elizabeth,

I always feel at peace if *you* like one of my garden pieces, so your letter was a great comfort and joy, except for the depressing news about your mother. I suppose you may soon have to make the agonizing decision whether or not to put her in a nursing home or hospital. I went through that particular hell when my ninety-two-year-old aunt came to live with us for good, after my sister, Rosamond, who lived in Sarasota, died... I do feel, though, that it is wrong for a younger person to lose her health and stop her work in order to care for someone who no longer gets anything out of having the younger person there. This probably is not so yet with your mother. Anyway, I am so sorry, dear Elizabeth. Every case is different and please do not think I would presume to suggest what you should do...

I would love to have the hellebore plant or plants if you can spare it or them. I don't think I should try bamboo this year— not until I figure where to put the thicket. I've recently discovered there is a clump just down the road hiding an outhouse, so perhaps I could get my root from there early next spring. The garden was a mess when I left—no rain just when we were transplanting annuals. I dread going back to it especially since I seem to have picked up sciatica in New York and will find working in a garden difficult...

Affectionately,

Katharine

P.S. I hope you're reading the Rachel Carson pieces, grim as they are.

July 3 [1962]

Dear Katharine,

I put the little Nandina seedling in with the hellebores, and a nice root of Ivy Fleur de lis that came up with the Nandina.

Promise you won't bother with these if they come at an inconvenient time. More will be forthcoming.

I remember you said you wished Mr. Ranger wouldn't bother you with ideas—so I try not to—but Ellen (Flood) sent me such an interesting brochure on organic gardening. It costs a dollar—but I'm sure he'll be only too glad to send it free—and comes from the Brookside Nurseries, Darien, Connecticut. Ellen went there to a demonstration, and was entranced with everything but the garbage compost. She says it *does* smell.

I wrote about *Silent Spring,* and I shall write again. I am also trying to see that everyone reads *The New Yorker.*

Thank you for your sympathy and concern. I am getting on better. I may come to the nursing home, as we continuously go beyond our income this way—but it would be much harder for me to have my mother there. My sister has taken a job for next winter, as she has two children in school next year. That will make it difficult, too.

I hope you are better. I know I have more to say, but I can't find your letter. I didn't file it and there is no telling what pile it is under.

Aff,

Elizabeth Lawrence

P.S. Fuzz says she will mail the plants for me.

. . .

July 13, 1962

Dear Elizabeth,

... The plants arrived in perfect shape and by some miracle Henry and I got them into the ground on a foggy, cloudy day. They've been watered constantly since then and look well. We are in the midst of what the paper calls the worst drought in ten years. Every time I water, I wonder whether the spring, which has never failed, will fail this time. We don't dare water the big vegetable garden so the peas are drying up on the vines and nothing grows. Mostly it's been sun, sun, sun but also we're way behind because the spring was so late.

I put the Nandina against the east side of the gray-shingled garage and shop. I fear it may not winter here but it will be fun to try it and with winter protection I hope it will live. It is wonderful to have the Hellebores, and the Ivy fleur de lis now growing in a big terra rossa pot filled with petunias on the terrace; I shall bring it indoors next winter. I'm ignorant on ivies. This one would not be hardy here, would it?

I cherish *ideas* more than anything, especially from you. What I said about Mr. Ranger must have been written in a pet when he sold me on buying an expensive book on old roses, which turned out to be only one in a series of which the remainder is unavailable...

This is a poor letter but I'll send it for there may be no chance to write a better one.

Ever gratefully,

Katharine

New York
August 6, 1962
Dear Elizabeth,

... Today [Andy] turned in the page proofs of his fall book. Working on them has been what I've been doing mostly. My hopes of doing a brief garden piece for late August or early September have been defeated and I suppose the garden itself has suffered by my absence. When I left home your plants all seemed to be doing nicely. The only garden news I've had is that our biggest, most important vine on the terrace windbreak shows sign of "clematis wilt." What *is* clematis wilt? And what does one do for it? This is our third attack in this location. The first time it struck, I dug up the vine, burned it, and changed the soil. Then I read in one of the reference books that all one needed to do was to cut off the vine at the ground and it would come up again. So I did this earlier this year on a new vine that turned brown. Now it looks to me like something contagious. Is it a fungus? I can't remember. Or is it another name for nematodes, or what? Maybe I'd better just get home fast and apply sugar or a nice sweet rice pudding!...

I met Mary Ellen Flood in the halls yesterday, looking thin and pretty and happy. Nice to see her.

Aff'y,

Katharine

P.S. Home—and a quick look at the gardens makes me realize how badly they have suffered from two summers of neglect. The long north border has very little bloom. But the sun has been absent for two and a half months.

[August 1962]

Dear Katherine,

I'm sorry the plants came in the drought. They left in cool, showery weather. I didn't suppose you were ever dry or hot. Don't fool with them. I can always send more in the fall—I don't expect the nandina to live—but I love to send things North. That is what we had—but I don't want to worry you. I doubt whether the ivy is hardy—but if you want to try it, I can always send more.

Elsie Hassan says that only one miniature rose has proved hardy in Ohio—"Leprechaun," I think—so they are not likely to be hardy with you.

Joseph Mitchell's sisters were here last week. Linda Lamm says she bought *Her Garden Was Her Delight* after reading your review. They came to their niece's wedding. Each bridesmaid carried an enormous, *absolutely perfect* magnolia. I don't know how they did it. Magnolias turn brown if you even *look* at them...

Aff,

Elizabeth Lawrence

P.S. Linda loved the "Onward and Upward."

We get sprayed regularly with DDT—our small lot, 225' deep, gets it *twice*, front and back in one night. I have all the symptoms of DDT poisoning: "extreme irritability—great distaste for work of any sort—a feeling of mental incompetence in tackling the simplest mental task—the joint pains are quite violet at times." I forgot to look in *The Gardener's Bug Book* to see about the clematis wilt. If you want to fumigate there is a whole paragraph—Nemafume, Dowfume, Soilfume, etc.! I thought you would be interested in the sugar cure—see page 3. Please return the Bulletin for my files. I try to join a new society each year, to write about in my column. The Boxwood Society is the newest! *The Daffodil Year Book* is excellent. Some of the best people are writing for it.

August 11, 1962
[Dear Katharine,]
The wilt is caused by a nematode, and as far as I know there is nothing to be done about it, that you have not done already.

The thing is, good culture-healthy plants don't succumb... My system is to grow only what shows.

I hope the luck has now changed. I know how you feel about the garden.

Aff,

E.L.

THE LAMENTATION
TREE

STANLEY KUNITZ

Stanley Kunitz (1905–2006) twice held the position of United States Poet Laureate, the second time at age ninety-five. The first of his twelve collections of poetry appeared in 1930; since then, he has won the Pulitzer and Bollingen poetry prizes, a National Medal of the Arts, and a National Book Award. A teacher and poetry consultant to the Library of Congress, he was once a farmer, and always a gardener. Until his death at a hundred, he gardened at his summer home on Cape Cod. In his final book, *The Wild Braid: A Poet Reflects on a Century in the Garden,* from which this excerpt is taken, he writes, "I think of gardening as an extension of one's own being, something as deeply personal and intimate as writing a poem."

. . .

WHEN WE FIRST moved in, there was a wild cherry tree, rather nondescript, growing there in a bed of ivy by the cellar door in front of the house. It was the only tree in the garden area, and, like most wild cherry trees, it was infested with gypsy moths and all sorts of destructive creatures. I managed to get rid of most of the visible insects, but the tree showed no signs of recovering and it was clear I was fighing a lost cause in trying to preserve it.

While digging to see what was causing all that devastation, I found that the roots were being devoured by root borers so I tried everything to get rid of them, and meanwhile the wild ivy kept growing. It seemed immune to the insects devouring the tree itself. And soon the ivy covered the whole tree and began dangling from it. In time the tree assumed the character of a woman locked in mourning.

Seeing the tree this way brought me back to my Bennington years, between 1946 and 1949. Martha Graham was there at that time and I was very interested in her work and often watched her classes. I remember in particular her saying to a group of dancers, "Stop! You all look so self-conscious, and self-consciousness is always ugly!"

She was trying to cultivate in them a sense of fluid movement and at the same time she was interested in far more than anatomical exercises. She tried to convey a sense of the mythological powers of the body.

One of her famous dances was called "Lamentation." She worked with her group of dancers to find a means of expressing lamentation through the postures of the body, centered in a very contracted torso, bending the body into a pattern that seemed to crystallize all the grief within the powers of the body to express without language. Gradually my ivy-burdened cherry tree seemed to take on the exact same posture. It was so bent over with the weight of its grief that it no longer reached toward the sky but toward the earth, and so I named it "The Lamentation Tree."

The ivy continued thriving, becoming heavier and heavier, killing off the last traces of life in the original tree. This was a period of frequent tropical storms and hurricanes late in the season, and the tree no longer seemed capable of resisting these high winds. In the late sixties, at the height of a hurricane that was battering us, the dying branches no longer could sustain its weight and the whole tree gave way.

I remember very well cutting it into pieces—it was rotted all the way through—and getting rid of it. Then the question remained, how was I going to give a new birth to that place? I settled on a Rose of Sharon called "The Bluebird." It seemed symbolic and mythically correct that a bluebird should succeed my lamentation tree, and it still is there and blossoms exuberantly every year.

The lamentation tree was the most conspicuous eccentricity in the garden during those early years. I've always regarded it as an allegory of the capacity for change in nature. That tree changed its character and took on a life of its own, transforming from a wild diseased cherry tree into something else, no longer a tree really, but something emblematic, mythological.

Part of the fascination of gardening is that it is, on the one hand, a practical exercise of the human body and, on the other, a direct participation in the ritual of birth and life and death.

PATIENCE AND GRACE

PATRICK LANE

Patrick Lane (1939–) is one of Canada's most acclaimed poets. He is the author of more than twenty books of poetry and most recently a memoir, *There is a Season* (2004). Published in the United States as *What the Stones Remember,* the book recounts the year Lane spent in his garden outside Victoria, British Columbia, recovering from a lifetime of alcohol and drug abuse and searching for the roots of his dependency. He brings to his garden not only the keen eye of a naturalist and a poet's sensitivity, but a lifetime of reading and experience traveling throughout the world. The half-acre garden, which he shares with poet Lorna Crozier, has been featured in the *Recreating Eden* television series.

. . .

I'VE BEEN HOME for a month and there is work to be done. Tools need to be seen to and plans have to be made. As these first weeks stretch out I have begun to feel a little stronger. My first

159

tentative reaching is now more sure, though there are moments when I stand alone by the bamboo and tremble like its leaves.

Everywhere are the gentle nuances of plants pushing delicately into the scant warmth of a sun a bare month or so past the solstice. Even on a grey day like this the air has a smell to it, or is it just that my hands are already covered in the wet mulch of earth? I can taste the earth quickening. The irises know. So do the skimmia. Their leaves are a brighter green and the red berries on the female glow in the muted light. They reflect in the pond beside the falling water as it burbles over the pitted sandstone. A second red shimmer in the dark water is a surface reflection of the aestivating fish sleeping at the bottom, their tails moving slowly as they wait for the warmer spring to come. They will begin to rise for food in late February, a little thinner than they were in October when they settled into the season of short days and long nights.

Patience, I say, be like the koi in deep water. There is a time for everything. The gardener knows his hours, just as the fish do. All things in this garden wait for the sun to climb higher. I must only remain aware and bring to my daily life the knowledge of sixty-odd years and the thousands more of the generations who taught me. Moving a single stone in my garden is a motion as old as the hands of my great-grandfather lifting a stone from a broken field in Alberta. Earth-knuckles, they rose like fists on the backs of ice.

I move from bed to bed, a bit of weeding, some pruning, a general cleanup of the day lilies and the any other leftovers from autumn. Lorna couldn't get to it all when I was away. This garden is a shared space and one gardener alone cannot keep up to its demands. I hesitate to clean too much in case of a rare snowfall or frost. Last year's leaves protect the sleeping flowers.

Patience, go slowly, stop and watch the squirrel attack the bird feeder by the woodpile. I have given up driving her away and now accept she has her own needs. What am I trying to save, a handful a day of sunflower seeds? I let her have her due. I enjoy her slender busyness, the way she scolds the cats if they get too close, the way she sits in the crotch of a fir branch four metres up and calmly pulls the seeds from her cheeks to shell and eat. She is as much a denizen of this place as the birds. Come late spring she will appear with a consort or even two. The ways of squirrels are fine with me. I delight in her long journey along the top of the fence, the precise path she takes from fence to fir to redwood to cedar and then gone down the block in her pursuit of whatever it is squirrels desire.

I squat on a cedar round by the pond and watch the many birds at their play. The crow of a few hours ago passes over, this time heading west. Is it the same crow? I recognize some of them from season to season because of their peculiar habits. One uses the bird bath to soak bits of meat from roadkills or chicken legs scavenged from garbage bags. She drops the bits of bone and cartilage into the bird bath all spring and summer long. The songbirds don't seem to mind and flail about among small floating islands of pork or chicken grease when she's gone. You'd think they would recognize the smell of another bird who

has been deep-fried, but they don't. I gave up long ago dissuad-
ing the crow from soaking her food. Who ever convinced a
crow to do other than what she wishes?

Her fledglings sometimes learn the trick, but it is her I recognize. She has two small white feathers in the helmet curve
above her left eye. It is the eye she stares at me with, as if to
say she knows exactly who I am and she does. After all, I'm the
gardener who fiddles and diddles about this patch of ground. "A
piece of land not so very large," "a little spot enclosed by grace,"
as Horace and Watts had it. I have it the same way.

I have to spray the fruit trees with dormant oil and lime sul-
phur. The insects have planted their eggs in the cracks and crannies. Some pruning needs to be done as well. The suckers are
a punk hairdo on the apple trees. The compost needs turning.
The detritus of autumn Lorna didn't have time to get to still lies
in piles on the other side of the house. It has to be barrowed over
to the truck and taken to the recycling depot. If I had been home
I would have done this weeks ago and now the piles are a wet
mess, a bed for sleeping slugs and sowbugs.

Procrastination is the gardener's worst enemy. The words
I'll do it next week can stretch time into months. Procrastination
was my constant companion in the years of drinking. Every task
became secondary to my desperation.

I don't like where the previous year's cuttings are dumped.
The east side of the house is narrow and heavily shaded. One
task this year is to turn it into a modest shade garden with ferns,
stone, and moss. Over the years it seems there was nowhere else
to pile the vegetation as it accumulated.

Time to cut some branches from the back of the forsythia and force them in a vase in the front hall. Their deep lemon-yellow flowers are a wonder in this earliest of months. There are already several flowers on the bush and the other buds strain toward blossoming. I will place a branch in the slender jar by the tub upstairs where Lorna bathes each morning. I try to keep a flower blooming there every day of the year. I love to see her in the bath with the seasonal blossoms beside her.

Colour in a garden is not the only thing to look for. Shapes are beautiful as well. The corkscrew hazel in the large blue pot beside the magnolia is a maze of arabesques against the cedar fence. Catkins hang from the tips of its branches. I want to touch them each time I pass by. The hazel is lovely at all seasons but particularly in winter after the leaves fall. It is then you see the net of branches as they spiral and curve.

Right now two slate juncos perch on its highest branches. Their pale grey backs and breasts are a complement to the shifting blue of the ceramic planter below them. They are as common in my garden as the Oregon juncos and seeing them today is a kind of blessing. Robins, varied thrushes, and rufous-sided towhees are eating the purple berries of the daphne that come ripe in spring, an early feast for the birds. The males storm about in mock fights while the females watch with seeming disregard as they feed. Robins are particularly aggressive and many fights come to blows and beaks as they explode in the branches of some tree or other. No wonder they are sometimes called the American robin. Like our neighbours to the south, they can be very belligerent. The towhees are much quieter. Their battles are mostly song with an occasional rush toward some other male who has wandered by chance onto the lawn. Such slight aggression rarely ends up in a fight, the lesser bird quickly vacating the garden.

The beauty of winter is a wonder and mostly because I have to look past the show of early bulbs to the other, less obvious delights. The corkscrew hazel is only one of many beauties here. Behind me water warbles from the tube of timber bamboo under the skimmia. The towhees and juncos love to go up to the falling water and sip from the tiny pools that have gathered in the piece of sandstone I found with my friend and fellow writer, Brian Brett, on a beach near Saltspring Island.

That is beauty, to stop a moment and watch the endless play of light on water and stone and see how the living things of the garden come to drink or just to gaze as I do now at the surface of the pond. The cats have a terrible time seeing past the reflections on the water. Both Basho and Roxy will sit by the pond and stare into it. When a fish rises they are shocked by the sudden presence of a life that exists below. They will extend a paw sometimes and touch the water as if they can't quite believe it.

Grace, patience, beauty, what else has come to mind on these January days? That seems enough for now.

A GARDENER'S CREDO

GERTRUDE JEKYLL

Gertrude Jekyll (1843–1932) began as a painter, then turned to garden design and writing in midlife, publishing her first book at fifty-six and writing another dozen before she died at eighty-nine. But she was always a gardener. Intensely curious about the natural world, she brought an artistic vision to her gardens, emphasizing color and texture. She spent most of her life in Surrey, England, particularly at Munstead Wood where she ran a garden and plant-breeding center. In all, she designed over four hundred gardens, many of which are now restored and open to the public. Her credo, as inspiring today as when it was written, comes from the introductory chapter to her first book, *Wood and Garden: Notes and Thoughts, Practical and Critical, of a Working Amateur* (1899).

. . .

I LAY NO CLAIM either to literary ability, or to botanical knowledge, or even to knowing the best practical methods of cultivation; but I have lived among outdoor flowers for many years, and have not spared myself in the way of actual labour, and have come to be on closely intimate and friendly terms with a great many growing things, and have acquired certain instincts which, though not clearly defined, are of the nature of useful knowledge.

But the lesson I have thoroughly learnt, and wish to pass on to others, is to know the enduring happiness that the love of a garden gives. I rejoice when I see any one, and especially children, inquiring about flowers, and wanting gardens of their own, and carefully working in them. For the love of gardening is a seed that once sown never dies, but always grows and grows to an enduring and ever-increasing source of happiness.

If in the following chapters I have laid special stress upon gardening for beautiful effect, it is because it is the way of gardening that I love best, and know most about, and that seems to me capable of giving the greatest amount of pleasure. I am strongly for treating garden and wooded ground in a pictorial way, mainly with large effects, and in the second place with lesser beautiful incidents, and for so arranging plants and trees and grassy spaces that they look happy and at home, and make no parade of conscious effort. I try for beauty and harmony everywhere, and especially for harmony of colour. A garden so treated gives the delightful feeling of repose, and refreshment, and purest enjoyment of beauty, that seems to my understanding to be the best fulfilment of its purpose; while to the diligent worker its happiness is like the offering of a constant hymn of praise. For I hold that the best purpose of a garden is to give delight and to give refreshment of mind, to soothe, to refine, and to lift up the heart in a spirit of praise and thankfulness. It is certain that those who practise gardening in the best ways find it to be so.

But the scope of practical gardening covers a range of horticultural practice wide enough to give play to every variety of human taste. Some find their greatest pleasure in collecting as large a number as possible of all sorts of plants from all sources, others in collecting them themselves in their foreign homes, others in making rock-gardens, or ferneries, or peat-gardens, or bog-gardens, or gardens for conifers or for flowering shrubs, or special gardens of plants and trees with variegated or coloured leaves, or in the cultivation of some particular race or family of plants. Others may best like wide lawns with large trees, or wild gardening, or a quite formal garden, with trim hedge and walk, and terrace, and brilliant parterre, or a combination of several ways of gardening. And all are right and reasonable and enjoyable to their owners, and in some way or degree helpful to others.

The way that seems to me most desirable is again different, and I have made an attempt to describe it in some of its aspects. But I have learned much, and am always learning, from other people's gardens, and the lesson I have learned most thoroughly is, never to say "I know"—there is so infinitely much to learn, and the conditions of different gardens vary so greatly, even when soil and situation appear to be alike and they are in the same district. Nature is such a subtle chemist that one never knows what she is about, or what surprises she may have in store for us.

Often one sees in the gardening papers discussions about the treatment of some particular plant. One man writes to say it can only be done one way, another to say it can only be done quite some other way, and the discussion waxes hot and almost angry, and the puzzled reader, perhaps as yet young in gardening, cannot tell what to make of it. And yet the two writers are both able gardeners, and both absolutely trustworthy, only they should have said, "In my experience *in this place* such a plant can only be done in such a way." Even plants of the same family will not do equally well in the same garden. Every practical gardener knows this is the case of strawberries and potatoes; he has to find out which kinds will do in his garden; the experience of his friend in the next county is probably of no use whatever.

I have learnt much from the little cottage gardens that help to make our English waysides the prettiest in the temperate world. One can hardly go into the smallest cottage garden without learning or observing something new. It may be some two plants growing beautifully together by some happy chance, or a pretty mixed tangle of creepers, or something that one always thought must have a south wall doing better on an east one. But eye and brain must be alert to receive the impression and studious to store it, to add to the hoard of experience. And it is important to train oneself to have a good flower-eye; to be able to see at a glance what flowers are good and which are unworthy, and why, and to keep an open mind about it; not to be swayed by the petty tyrannies of the "florist" or show judge; for, though some part of his judgment may be sound, he is himself a slave to rules, and must go by points which are defined arbitrarily and rigidly, and have reference mainly to the show-table, leaving out of account, as if unworthy of consideration, such matters as gardens and garden beauty, and human delight, and sunshine, and varying lights of morning and evening and noonday. But many, both nurserymen and private people, devote themselves to growing and improving the best classes of hardy flowers, and we can hardly offer them too much praise, or do them too much honour. For what would our gardens be without the Roses, Paeonies, and Gladiolus of France, and the Tulips and Hyacinths of Holland, to say nothing of the hosts of good things raised by our home growers, and of the enterprise of the great firms whose agents are always searching the world for garden treasures?

Let no one be discouraged by the thought of how much there is to learn. Looking back upon nearly thirty years of gardening (the earlier part of it in groping ignorance with scant means of help), I can remember no part of it that was not full of pleasure and encouragement. For the first steps are steps into a delightful Unknown, the first successes are victories all the happier for being scarcely expected, and with the growing knowledge comes the widening outlook, and the comforting sense of an ever-increasing gain of criticial appreciation. Each new step becomes a little surer, and each new grasp a little firmer, till, little by little, comes the power of intelligent combination, the nearest thing we can know to the mighty force of creation.

And a garden is a grand teacher. It teaches patience and careful watchfulness; it teaches industry and thrift; above all, it teaches entire trust. "Paul planteth and Apollos watereth, but God giveth the increase." The good gardener knows with absolute certainty that if he does his part, if he gives the labour, the love, and every aid that his knowledge of his craft, experience of the conditions of his place, and exercise of his personal wit can work together to suggest, that so surely as he does this diligently and faithfully, so surely will God give the increase. Then with the honestly-earned success comes the consciousness of encouragement to renewed effort, and, as it were, an echo of the gracious words, "Well done, good and faithful servant."

ACKNOWLEDGMENTS

"Bringing Home the Regal Lily" excerpted from *Plant Hunting* (1927) by Ernest H. Wilson, published in *The Gardener's World* edited by Joseph Wood Krutch. (New York: G. P. Putnam's Sons, 1959).

"The Transvaal Daisy" excerpted from *Some Flowers* by Vita Sackville-West. (London, England: Cobden-Sanderson, 1937).

"Monet's Garden" excerpted from *My Garden (Book):* by Jamaica Kincaid. (New York: Farrar Straus Giroux, 1999).

"The Green Shroud" excerpted from *The Lost Gardens of Heligan* by Tim Smit. (London: Weidenfled & Nicolson, a division of The Orion Publishing Group Ltd, 2000.)

"On Reading a Garden" excerpted from *Stonyground: The Making of a Canadian Garden* by Douglas Chambers. (Toronto: Alfred A. Knopf Canada, 1996).

"The First Garden" excerpted from *Tottering in My Garden: A Gardener's Memoir with Notes for the Novice* by Midge Ellis Keeble. Copyright © 1989, 1994 by Midge Keeble. All rights reserved. Reprinted by permission of Firefly Books Ltd. (Toronto: Camden House, 1989).

"Right Good Ground" excerpted from *Book Seventeen, Chapter five of The Historie of the World: Commonly called, The Naturall Historie of C. Plinius Secundus*, translated by Philemon Holland. (London: Adam Islip, 1634).

"Preparations" excerpted from *The Gardener's Year* by Karel Capek, translated by M. and R. Weatherall. (Wisconsin: The University of Wisconsin Press, 1984).

"A German Garden" excerpted from *Elizabeth and her German Garden* by Elizabeth von Arnim. (London: The Macmillan Company, 1900).

"Captive Gardens" excerpted from *Le Voyage Égoiste in Oeuvres Complètes de Colette*. (Paris: Le Fleuron, 1949). English translation by Merilyn Simonds, 2007.

"Blitz Flowers" by Lewis Gannett, first published in the *New York Herald Tribune*, 1944, anthologized in *The Gardener's World*, edited by Joseph Wood Krutch. (New York: G.P. Putnam's Sons, 1959).

"The Purest of Pleasures" excerpted from *The Essays; or, Counsels, Civil and Moral of Francis Bacon*. (New York: A. L. Burt, Publisher, 1883). Originally published 1625.

"On Supplanting Rampant Nettledom" excerpted from *Elizabeth's Garden: Elizabeth Smart on the Art of Gardening*, edited by Alice Van Wart. (Toronto: Coach House Press, © Sebastian Barker, 1989).

"A Snake in the Garden" excerpted from *A Garden Diary: September 1899–September 1900* by Emily Lawless. (London: Methuen & Co., 1901).

"Invasion of the Sumac" excerpted from *Farther Afield: A Gardener's Excursions* by Allen Lacy. (New York: Farrar Straus Giroux, 1981).

"The Revolting Garden" excerpted from *The Revolting Garden* by Rose Blight. (London: Private Eye/André Deutsch, 1979).

"On the Rootedness of Plants," excerpted from *Our Gardens, Ourselves: Reflections on an Ancient Art* by Jennifer Bennett. (Toronto: Camden House Press, 1994).

"Thomas Hardy in his Garden" excerpted from *Thomas Hardy in his Garden* by Bertie Norman Stephens. (Dorset: J. Stevens Cox, Beaminster, 1963).

"On Beauty" excerpted from *Conversations with My Gardener* by Henri Cueco, translated by George Miller. (London: Granta Books, 2005).

"Sex, Sex, Sex" excerpted from *Anatomy of a Rose* by Sharman Apt Russell. Reprinted by permission of Basic Books, a member of Perseus Books Group. (Cambridge: Perseus Publishing, 2001).

"Peonies" excerpted from *Green Thoughts* by Eleanor Perenyi, Copyright © 1981 by Eleanor Perenyi. Used by permission of Random House, Inc.

"Poppycock" excerpted from *An Ecology of Enchantment: A Year in a Country Garden* by Des Kennedy. (Toronto: Harper Collins, 1988). Reprinted by permission of the author.

"A Few Hints on Gardening" excerpted from *The Canadian Settler's Guide* by Mrs. C.P. Traill. (Toronto: the Old Countryman Office, 1855).

The David Suzuki Foundation works through science and education to protect the diversity of nature and our quality of life, now and for the future.

With a goal of achieving sustainability within a generation, the Foundation collaborates with scientists, business and industry, academia, government and non-governmental organizations. We seek the best research to provide innovative solutions that will help build a clean, competitive economy that does not threaten the natural services that support all life.

The Foundation is a federally registered independent charity, which is supported with the help of over 50,000 individual donors across Canada and around the world.

We invite you to become a member. For more information on how you can support our work, please contact us:

The David Suzuki Foundation

219–2211 West 4th Avenue

Vancouver, BC

Canada v6k 4s2

www.davidsuzuki.org

contact@davidsuzuki.org

Tel: 604-732-4228 · Fax: 604-732-0752

Checks can be made payable to The David Suzuki Foundation.
All donations are tax-deductible.
Canadian charitable registration: (BN) 12775 6716 RR0001
U.S. charitable registration: #94-3204049